A MUSICAL BOOK OF DAYS

A MUSICAL
BOOK OF DAYS

NORMAN LEBRECHT

UNIVERSE BOOKS
New York

Published in the United States of America in 1989
by Universe
300 Park Avenue South, New York, NY 10010
Copyright © Norman Lebrecht

91 92 93 / 10 9 8 7 6 5 4 3 2

Printed in the United States of America

Library of Congress Cataloging-in-Publication Data
Lebrecht, Norman, 1948–
    A musical book of days / Norman Lebrecht.
      p.   cm.
    Reprint. Originally published: London : Collins, 1987.
    ISBN 0-87663-684-9
    1. Music–Biography. 2. Music–Quotations, maxims, etc.
3. Birthday Books.   I. Title.
ML66.L3   1989
780'.9 – dc19   88-36524
                                                CIP
                                                MN

For
NICOLAS SLONIMSKY;
father of musical chronography,
born
27 April 1894
in St Petersburg
and still going strong
in Los Angeles.

INTRODUCTION

Music and musicians are unnaturally obsessed with anniversaries. Concert planners constantly scan history for the faintest hint of a centenary, a jubilee or a birthday around which a programme, festival or multi-media jamboree can be staged. No matter how dubious the date or insignificant the instance, the mere sight of the mystic formula '100 years since . . .' triggers a Pavlovian response in box-office queues.

This fascination with calendrical coincidence is unique to the musical world; it scarcely touches the other arts. Nor is it readily explained, though its origins must lie somewhere in the common cerebral roots of music and mathematics.

The Musical Book of Days celebrates this harmless obsession with a kaleidoscope of compositional events, experiences and expletives for every day of the year. Culled from 14 centuries of occidental concord and occasional dissonance, it spotlights isolated moments in the performing and private lives of great musicians. Trivial or tremendous, sublime or simply scandalous, the daily incidents form their own miniature portraits of music in its making.

Although entries have been carefully validated, absolute accuracy is humanly unattainable. Reports of any errors found will be gratefully received and the offence amended in future editions.

The dates conform as a rule with *The New Grove Dictionary of Music and Musicians* (Macmillan, 1980), or with Nicolas Slonimsky's *Music since 1900* (Scribners, 1937 *et seq.*), except when contradicted by primary sources. Pre-1917 Russian dates are given in the Western equivalent, but English dates before 1751 have not been Europeanised. All performances

7

are world premieres, unless otherwise indicated.

Dates of death outnumber those of births, because last words carry more weight than first and accomplishment is more impressive than mere promise. Or, as the Solomonian proverb put it: 'A good name is better than precious ointment; and the day of death than the day of one's birth' (Ecc. VII, 1). By a reverse bias, debuts are preferred to farewell performances – unless they happen to be one and the same.

1 JANUARY

J * A * N * U * A * R * Y

1 JANUARY

1782 Johann Christian Bach dies in Paddington, aged 46. The 'London Bach', Johann Sebastian's youngest son, leaves debts of £4,000 and is commemorated in the andante of Mozart's 12th piano concerto.

1791 At 5 p.m. at Dover, Joseph Haydn sets foot on English soil.
'Haydn! Great Sovereign of the tuneful art!
Thy works alone supply an ample chart
Of all the mountains, seas and fertile plains
Within the compass of its wide domains –
Is there an Artist of the present day
Untaught by thee to think as well as play?'[1]

1853 'I shall have *La Dame aux Camélias* performed in Venice. It will perhaps be called *La Traviata*' – Verdi, to a friend.

1855 'I have worked out in my mind a *Tristan and Isolde*, the simplest yet the most full-blooded musical conception; and at the end, when the "black flag" is hoisted, I shall cover myself with it and die' – Wagner to Liszt.

1865 Berlioz ends his memoirs: 'I can die now without anger or bitterness.'

1869 'Early in the morning the Friend came to greet me and wish me a happy New Year. ... The Friend has given me the golden pen with which he wrote *Tristan* and *Siegfried*. ... the pen which has traced the sublimest things ever created by a noble spirit shall now be dedicated solely to the depths of a woman's heart' – Cosima, Liszt's daughter, begins her diary of life with Richard Wagner.

1879 Brahms' concerto for violin – opponents call it 'concerto *against* the violin' – is performed at Leipzig by his friend Joseph Joachim.

1908 Gustav Mahler makes his US debut at the Metropolitan Opera, conducting *Tristan and Isolde*.

1909 A multi-million dollar New York insurance agency, Ives & Myrick, is co-founded by America's most inventive composer, Charles E. Ives.

1913 Louis Armstrong, 13, is arrested and sent to a boys' home for firing his step-father's shotgun during New Year celebrations.

1945 Iannis Xenakis loses an eye and nearly his life in street fighting while leading a Resistance unit in Athens.

1988 *New Year*, Michael Tippett's fifth opera, nears completion.

[1]Welcoming doggerel by Charles Burney.

1843 Wagner presents *The Flying Dutchman*, his first mature opera, an idea that came to him while sheltering from a storm in a Norwegian fjord.

1874 Two days after finishing his Third Symphony, Anton Bruckner starts the Fourth.

1905 Michael Tippett is born in London, second son of a lawyer-turned-businessman and a militant suffragette.

Wandering Wagner

1958 Maria Callas provokes uproar in Rome, pulling out after one act of *Norma* with 'inflammation of the vocal cords'. Late the night before she was seen dancing in the New Year. 'In the interests of public order', she is banned from re-entering Rome Opera. She sues, winning 2.7 million lire restitution.

1785 Death of Baldassare Galuppi, Venetian composer.

> 'Oh Galuppi, Baldassaro, this is very sad to find!
> I can hardly misconceive you; it would prove me deaf and blind;
> But although I take your meaning, 'tis with such a heavy mind!

> 'Here you come with your old music, and here's all the good it brings.
> What, they lived once thus at Venice where the merchants were the kings,
> Where Saint Mark's is, where the Doges used to wed the sea with rings?'[1]

1843 Donizetti's *Don Pasquale*, his final success, is staged in Paris.

[1] Robert Browning, 'A Toccata of Galuppi's', 1847.

1868 Verdi plays billiards at home with his wife: 'He found nothing to criticise or to scold! ... Why isn't he always like that?'

1941 Rachmaninov's *Symphonic Dances*, his valedictory work for orchestra, is conducted in Philadelphia by Eugene Ormandy.

1710 Pergolesi is born at Iesi, grandson of a shoemaker of Pergola.

1916 Debussy: 'I have just seen Stravinsky. He says my *Firebird*, my *Sacre*, just as a child would say, my top, my hoop, and that's just what he is: a spoilt child who wears rowdy ties and kisses a lady's hand while stepping on her feet.'

1970 Maestro and Mrs Leonard Bernstein host a party at their Park Avenue penthouse for the Black Panther Defence Fund ... the sort of elegant slumming that degrades patrons and patronised alike' (*New York Times* editorial).

 **2 JANUARY**

 3 JANUARY

 4 JANUARY

5 JANUARY

 6 JANUARY

 7 JANUARY

1875 Before attending a Christmas Eve party[1] Peter Ilyich Tchaikovsky plays his B flat minor piano concerto to his former teacher, Nikolay Rubinstein, and two other friends. 'I played the first movement. Not a word, not a single remark ... For God's sake say *something*! But Rubinstein never opened his lips. He was preparing his thunderbolt ... I gathered patience and played the concerto through to the end. Still silence. "Well?" I asked, getting up from the piano. A torrent burst from Nikolay Grigorevich's lips, gently at first, gaining volume and finally exploding into the tone of Jove the Thunderer. My concerto was worthless, utterly unplayable. The passages were broken, awkward and so ineptly written that they could not be put right. The work itself was bad, trivial and common; here and there I had stolen from other people. Only one or two pages were worth anything at all; the rest should be destroyed or completely rewritten ...'

1931 Pianist Alfred Brendel is born at Wiesenberg, Moravia.

1932 Ravel's concerto for left hand is played in Vienna by Paul Wittgenstein, a wealthy pianist who lost his right arm in the First War.

[1]The Russian Christmas falls on January 6.

1735 The closing section of Bach's *Christmas Oratorio* is sung in Leipzig on the Feast of the Epiphany.

1839 More than ten years after Schubert's death, Schumann 'gazes with astonishment' at five unpublished symphonies, several operas and four large masses. He offers to prepare a two-piano version of the symphonies but publishers are unenthusiastic.

1872 On Christmas Day, 'a coincidence to which he ascribes some special mystical significance', at 2 p.m. in Moscow, the composer Alexander Scriabin enters the world.

1809 'No-one in Vienna has more private enemies than I. This is easier to understand since the state of music here is getting worse and worse' – Beethoven to his publisher; he has lately performed the fifth and sixth symphonies.

1924 George Gershwin starts writing *Rhapsody in Blue* as a piece for two pianos.

1955 Marian Anderson, 53, as Ulrica in Verdi's *Un ballo in maschera*, becomes the first black person to sing at the Met.

1687 Beating time in his *Te Deum* to celebrate the Sun King's recovery from surgery, Jean-Baptiste Lully strikes his staff so heavily on his foot that gangrene fatally sets in.

1713 Arcangelo Corelli, leaving his valuable art collection to Cardinal Ottoboni, dies in Rome aged 59. 'A musician leaving money to a cardinal while he had a relation or necessitous friend in the world seems to savour more of vanity than true generosity,' writes Charles Burney.

1923 Opera is broadcast for the first time – *The Magic Flute* from Covent Garden by the BBC.

1970 Hours before his 44th birthday, Greek composer Jani Christou perishes in an Athens car smash, his opera on the *Oresteia* unconcluded.

1972 The fifteenth and final symphony by Dmitri Shostakovich is conducted in Moscow by his son, Maxim.

1850 Jenny Lind, the Swedish Nightingale who abandoned opera for religious reasons, signs a six-figure contract for a US tour with Phineas T. Barnum, circus promoter.

1928 Eugène Lemaire, 73, Parisian composer of operetta, ends it all in the Seine.

Six-figure Lind

1939 Béla Bartók, Benny Goodman and the violinist Josef Szigeti appear together in *Contrasts*, commissioned by the jazz clarinettist though too long for the single disc he wants to make.

1893 In New York, where he has been brought to teach, Dvořák starts work on his symphony *From the New World*.

1931 Nicolas Slonimsky introduces Ives' *Three Places in New England* in Boston. 'I developed a method of conducting two different beats simultaneously, one with the right hand and one with the left ... I believe this was the first time when a really stereophonic, or rather bilateral, type of music was played.'

1964 'The geography of the orchestra as it now exists is of no further interest' – Pierre Boulez directs *Figures Doubles Prismes* in Basle.

8 JANUARY

 9 JANUARY

 10 JANUARY

11 JANUARY

12 JANUARY

13 JANUARY

1863 Bizet's music is heard for the first time in concert, 'badly played, badly listened to, falling upon general inattention and indifference.'

1919 Having smuggled the score inside his trousers for fear its hieroglyphics might suggest a spy code to French border officials, Frederick Delius hears his *Eventyr* performed in London.

1925 Aaron Copland's symphony is hissed in New York; its conductor, Walter Damrosch, announces that 'if a young man at the age of 23 can write a symphony like that, in five years he will be ready to commit murder.'

1519 Death of Maximilian 1, Holy Roman Emperor and patron of art.
> Who will give our eyes
> a fountain of tears,
> that we shall weep
> before the Lord?
> Germany, what do you
> grieve?
> Music, why are you silent
> Austria, why do you
> waste away in grief,
> clothed in mourning?
> Alas, O Lord, Maximilian has left us . . .

1723 Handel, half-taming two sopranos, presents *Ottone*. He offers to suspend Francesca Cuzzoni out of the window until she emits a slow aria, *'Falsa imagine'*, but has less success with Anastasia Robinson, untitled Countess of Peterborough (the elderly Earl married her secretly but does not announce it for a dozen years). She protests to the Modenese Ambassador that 'fury and passion' arias are not her forte and Handel is forced to scrap one of her songs and reset another.

1928 Each making his New York debut, pianist Vladimir Horowitz and conductor Sir Thomas Beecham adopt irreconcilable tempi in the Tchaikovsky concerto, with predictable consequences.

1822 Beethoven concludes his final piano sonata, Op. 111, then decides that 'the pianoforte is, after all, an unsatisfactory instrument'.

1864 Stephen Collins Foster, America's songmaster, dies of concussion sustained while drunkenly banging his head on a chamber pot in a Bowery hotel room. He is 37.

1938 An electronic keyboard producing microtones is patented by Maurice Martenot. His 'Ondes Martenot' is played in Messiaen's *Turangaglila* symphony, and in works by Varèse, Milhaud, Honegger and Boulez.

1945 Prokofiev directs his Fifth Symphony, Op. 100, in Moscow. A few days afterwards he falls, is concussed and cannot conduct again.

1792 The spurious, amorous memoirs of soprano Elizabeth Billington, whom Haydn likens to an angel, sell out by 3 p.m. on publication day.

1900 *Tosca* opens the operatic century in Rome, marred by a bomb scare and threats to the singers from local musicians jealous of Puccini.

1932 Ravel's G major, his second piano concerto in ten days, is played in Paris by Marguerite Long.

1966 *A Jewish Chronicle* by composers from both Germanies – Dessau and Wagner-Régeny from the East; Blacher, Hartmann and Henze from the West – warning against revived anti-semitism, is performed in Cologne. 'We remembered how too often in the past artists had kept their own counsel, and how disastrous their silence had often been in the Third Reich,' writes Hans Werner Henze.

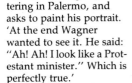

1864 Isaac Nathan, 74, sometimes called 'Father of Australian Music', is crushed by a Sydney tramcar.

1882 Auguste Renoir calls on Richard Wagner, wintering in Palermo, and asks to paint his portrait. 'At the end Wagner wanted to see it. He said: "Ah! Ah! I look like a Protestant minister." Which is perfectly true.'

1890 Tchaikovsky's *Sleeping Beauty* is danced in St Petersburg.

1907 Charmed by the music in a barber's shop on Capri, Sir Edward Elgar sketches an Andantino for mandolin, violin and guitar, while waiting for a haircut.

1941 In prisoner-of-war Stalag VIIIA at Görlitz in Silesia, Olivier Messiaen leads three fellow-inmates in his *Quartet for the end of time*.

1888 Gabriel Fauré directs his *Requiem* – 'composed for *nothing* ... for fun' – in its initial chamber version at the La Madeleine funeral of a rich man he did not know.

1920 The title *Les Six*, embracing the young Parisians Auric, Durey, Honegger, Milhaud, Poulenc and Germaine Tailleferre, is conferred on them by the critic Henri Collet: 'Their splendid decision to return to simplicity [has] brought about a renaissance of French music, by appreciating the phenomenon of Erik Satie and following the precepts, so lucid, of Jean Cocteau.'

1957 Two months before his 90th birthday, Arturo Toscanini, 'the supreme master of all conductors', dies in New York. 'I am no genius. I have created nothing. I play the music of other men. I am just a musician.'

14 JANUARY

 15 JANUARY

 16 JANUARY

 **17 JANUARY**

 18 JANUARY

 19 JANUARY

1751 Tomaso Albinoni, unjustly famed for an *adagio* devised by his biographer Giazotto, meets death in Venice aged 79.

1914 Erik Satie writes a ten-bar *Choral hypocrite* for violin and piano.

1919 Ignacy Jan Paderewski, 58, pianist, composer and patriot, is installed as the first Prime Minister of independent Poland. He resigns within the year and spends the rest of his days abroad.

Satie

1934 Einstein plays second fiddle, relatively speaking, in a performance of the Bach double concerto at a New York fundraiser for Nazi-oppressed scientists.

1835 César Cui, fifth and feeblest of Russia's 'Mighty Five' composers, emerges at Vilna, son of a French officer who failed to follow Napoleon's retreat.

1895 Richard Strauss begs Verdi, 'the true master of Italian lyric drama, to accept as a mark of homage and admiration a copy of *Guntram*, my first attempt in that genre ...'

1953 Aaron Copland's *Lincoln Portrait*, intended for the presidential inauguration of Dwight D. Eisenhower, is summarily scrapped. 'The Republican Party would have been ridiculed from one end of the US to the other if Copland's music had been played at the inaugural of a President elected to fight Communism, among other things,' declares Congressman Fred E. Busby (Illinois).

1576 Hans Sachs, Wagner's original mastersinger, dies in Nuremburg aged 81.

1853 Despite the Tiber's flooding, *Il Trovatore* triumphs. 'The Roman streets, which had once resounded to the cries of tribunes and triumvirs, re-echoed to the name of this Caesar in art, Verdi ... People even went to the theatre to look at the bare walls,' (Blanche Roosevelt: *Verdi, Milan and Otello*, 1887).

1911 Conducting 'The Stars and Stripes Forever' at Merthyr Tydfil, Wales, its composer John Philip Sousa falls seven feet through the floor. Re-emerging, he announces, 'We will now continue.'

1955 Simon Rattle, conductor, is born in Liverpool.

1851 At the opening of *Die Opernprobe* [The Opera Rehearsal], its composer Albert Lortzing, 49, collapses and dies.

1870 Guillaume Lekeu – 'I would kill myself to put all my soul in my music' – is born at Heusy, Belgium.

1876 Josef Hofmann, pianistic prodigy who in 1887 becomes the first recording musician, enters the world at Cracow.

1888 Gustav Mahler conducts his completion of Carl Maria von Weber's *Die Drei Pintos* while plotting to elope with the composer's granddaughter-in-law, Marion.

1894 Guillaume Lekeu, 24, composer of a brilliant violin sonata and incomplete piano quartet, dies of typhoid after eating contaminated sherbet; a loss, says an American critic, 'more tragic than that of Schubert or Pergolesi.'

1904 At the age of 49, Leoš Janáček sees his masterpiece *Jenůfa* acclaimed at provincial Brno but waits thirteen years before Prague accepts the opera.

1941 Placido Domingo, tenor, draws breath in Madrid.

1943 Béla Bartók, in his last concert appearance, disconcerts his wife in the premiere of his Concerto* for Two Pianos and Percussion by drifting off vaguely on a trail of his own improvisations.

* This is the concerto for two pianos – title usually omits the percussion – made from the earlier sonata.

1883 Bruckner begins the resplendent Adagio of his Seventh Symphony. 'I came home and felt very sad. The thought had entered my mind that before long the Master [Wagner] would die, and then the C-sharp minor theme of the Adagio came to me.'

1964 In an altercation with three French sailors in a Martinique bar, Marc Biltzstein, 59, leftist US composer, is battered to death.

Bruckner's beat

1969 Modernist Pierre Boulez is named principal conductor of the BBC Symphony Orchestra in London; six months later he takes over the New York Philharmonic. 'In politics you call this "entryism". One cannot forever bark outside like a dog.' (Boulez/NL).

20 JANUARY

 **21 JANUARY**

 **22 JANUARY**

23 JANUARY

 24 JANUARY

 **25 JANUARY**

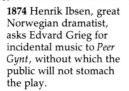

1837 John Field, 54, Irishman who invented the nocturne and taught the founders of Russian music, dies in Moscow.

1874 Henrik Ibsen, great Norwegian dramatist, asks Edvard Grieg for incidental music to *Peer Gynt*, without which the public will not stomach the play.

1908 At the Westminster Hotel, New York, after a period of mental decline, Edward Macdowell, 47, 'the American Grieg', gently fades away.

1922 Arthur Nikisch, the conductor Berlin called 'the Magician' and the first to record a complete symphony (Beethoven's 5th, 1913), dies at Leipzig aged 66.

17— 'About noon on St John Chrysostom's Day, a creature was born which had a face, hands and feet. Father, who was eating pea-soup at the time, was so overjoyed that he spilt a whole spoonful over his beard, whereupon the midwife laughed uproariously, causing all the strings of the lutenist's instrument to break in the middle of his latest lullaby.' E. T. A. Hoffmann introduces Kapellmeister Kreisler, archetype musician of the Romantic era.

1777 Christian Friedrich Daniel Schubart, loose-living poet and musician, author of *Die Forelle* (*The Trout*) and other verses set by Franz Schubert, begins a ten-year confinement in the dungeons of Duke Karl Eugen of Württemberg, whom he has offended in print. He passes the time writing *Ideas on the Aesthetics of Music*.

1922 In the drawing room of the Sitwells' house at 2 Carlyle Square, upper-crust London is shocked by an 'entertainment':

> FAÇADE
> Miss Edith Sitwell
> on her
> Sengerphone
> with accompaniments,
> overture and interlude
> by
> W. T. Walton.

1817 Cinderella becomes an opera for the third time in Rossini's *La Cenerentola*, staged in Rome.

1844 Mendelssohn's *Hear my Prayer* is heard in London.

1902 Franz Schmidt, a cellist in the Vienna Philharmonic, is hailed as 'a full-blooded, fresh talent [whose] open and honest nature won over the audience in no time' when he conducts his First Symphony.

1909 *Elektra*, bloodcurdling one-acter by Richard Strauss, is staged at Dresden.

1913 Witold Lutoslawski is born in Warsaw. 'I want to find ... people who in the depths of their souls feel the same way I do ... I regard creative activity as a kind of "soul-fishing", and the "catch" is the best medicine for loneliness, that most human of sufferings.'

1712 The first Giacomo Puccini, father of seven generations of composers, is born at Lucca.

1790 On the eve of his penultimate birthday, Mozart stages his third Da Ponte opera, *Cosi fan tutte*.

1867 Cora Pearl, an English courtesan with 'such a talent for voluptuous eccentricities that Prince G. described her as the acme of sensual delight' sings Cupidon in Offenbach's *Orpheus in the Underworld* at the Bouffes Parisiennes. Her tiny voice is tolerated by upper-crust males alert to other charms, but after a dozen nights students hoot her off.

1911 At Dresden, Richard Strauss achieves his greatest popular success in *Der Rosenkavalier*, Hofmannsthal's comedy of Viennese manners.

1922 Adrian Boult performs Vaughan Williams' *Pastoral Symphony*, his third, 'in four movements, all slow, so no-one will like it.'

1756 Johannes Chrysostomus Wolfgangus Theophilus Mozart opens his eyes at 8 p.m. in Salzburg, seventh and last child (but only the second to survive) of the Prince-Archbishop's deputy Kapellmeister, Leopold Mozart, himself the son of a bookbinder.

1895 Richard Strauss hears from Verdi: 'I have not had time to read your score, but from dipping into it I have seen that *Guntram* is the work of a very expert hand.'

1901 At 2.30 a.m. in a hotel suite in Milan, Verdi's life comes to an end. He is 87.
   'Let mourning and
      hope echo forth:
   He died and wept for
      all men.'
(Gabriele D'Annunzio).

1846 Three Paris specialists certify Donizetti as insane: '... The excitement of his genital organs no longer allows M. Donizetti to resist the impulse of his desires ...'

1926 Kurt Weill weds Lotte Lenya. 'She is a terrible housewife but a wonderful actress. She can't read a note of music but when she sings it sounds like Caruso (besides, I feel sorry for those composers whose wives read music). She takes no notice of my work but would be furious if I did not show an interest in hers.'

1936 In an article said to have been dictated by Stalin, *Pravda*, organ of the Communist Party of the USSR, excoriates Shostakovich's opera *Lady Macbeth of Mtsensk* under the headline:
CHAOS INSTEAD OF MUSIC
This game may end badly ... Shostakovich's opera is utterly devoid of political meaning; it titillates the perverted tastes of the bourgeoisie with its fidgeting, screaming, neurasthenic music.'

26 JANUARY

 27 JANUARY

 28 JANUARY

 **29 JANUARY**

 30 JANUARY

 31 JANUARY

1728 *The Beggar's Opera*, John Gay's ballad opera of London low-life, opens at John Rich's Lincoln's Inn Fields Theatre, making, it is quipped, 'Rich gay and Gay rich.' With the profits, Gay builds the first Covent Garden Theatre at Bow Street.

1877 'I am deaf and shall probably remain so forever ... You spoke of the ovations accorded me at the first performance of my latest opera, *The Kiss*, ovations such as I have never yet experienced, a reward for my attempts to introduce our national music into opera ... Unfortunately I was the only one in the packed house who did not hear a single note of the music, my own music' – Smetana, 52, to a former pupil.

1916 Prokofiev in Petrograd conducts his *Scythian Suite*. 'Just because I have a sick wife and three children,' moans a cellist, 'must I be forced to suffer this hell?'

1901 At dawn, according to his wishes, Verdi's body is taken secretly and buried in a temporary grave.

1917 Oscar Wilde's *A Florentine Tragedy*, once contemplated by Puccini, succeeds at Stuttgart as an opera by Alexander Zemlinsky.

1963 Francis Poulenc, 64, is felled in Paris by a heart attack. 'Like his name he was both dapper and ungainly ... His social predilections were for duchesses and policemen,' (Obituary by Ned Rorem).

1797 Franz Schubert is the first major composer to be born in Vienna. The next is Schoenberg.

1877 'Balakirev, dear gifted Balakirev, has risen from the dead and is alive for music.' After a five-year depression relieved by conversion to a singularly bigoted form of Russian Orthodoxy, the composer resumes the symphonic poem *Tamara* where he left off.

1881 'You will wonder how a man who is successful in his work can still complain and rail at fate? But my successes are not as important as they seem; they do not compensate for the intolerable sufferings I undergo when I mix in the society of my fellow-creatures' – Tchaikovsky to his benefactress, Nadezhda von Meck.

1937 Philip Glass, operatic minimalist, makes his entrance in Baltimore.

F * E * B * R * U * A * R * Y

1 FEBRUARY

1893 *Manon Lescaut*, Puccini's third opera and first success, opens at Turin, where in ...

1896 ... Toscanini premieres *La Bohème*, his next.

1930 *Von Heute auf Morgen*, a comedy of marital infidelity by Arnold Schoenberg and his wife Gertrud, is staged in Frankfurt, William Steinberg conducting. 'The difference', says Schoenberg, 'between what you played tonight and what I actually wrote in my score would make a new opera.'

1954 Hearing his Eighth Symphony, the first time his music is played in London for over 40 years, Havergal Brian, 78, is roused to compose a further 24 symphonies.

2 FEBRUARY

1594 Giovanni Pierluigi da Palestrina, 68, departs this earthly life in Rome. At the bedside of the great church composer stands Saint Philip Neri, in whose chapel (or oratory) the oratorio originated.

1875 Fritz Kreisler is born in Vienna and, aged 4, given a toy fiddle. 'One evening as [Father's quartet] were playing the national anthem the others stopped quite suddenly but I, engrossed in

my performance, continued in perfect time and tune ... It was decided then and there that I was a musical "marvel".'

1900 Charpentier's cohabitational opera *Louise* proves so popular that with the profits he sets up a musical conservatory for working girls like his unhappy seamstress heroine.

1901 Jascha Heifetz bows in at Vilna, Lithuania.

1905 Rachmaninov, Chaliapin and 27 other Moscow musicians publish an open letter deploring the massacre of demonstrators outside the Tsar's Winter Palace. 'There is only one solution: Russia must at last embark on a road of basic reforms.'

A composer called February, Henri Février (1875–1957), makes a successful opera of Maeterlinck's *Monna Vanna*, the tale of a Pisan general who sends his wife out in her nightie to placate the commander of the besieging Florentines. Rachmaninov starts composing the same text but finds that Février owns exclusive rights and will defend them. Dejected, he gives up opera for good.

 1 FEBRUARY

 2 FEBRUARY

 **3 FEBRUARY**

 4 FEBRUARY

 **5 FEBRUARY**

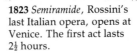

1818 Beethoven (in schoolboy French) to an English piano manufacturer: 'My very dear friend Broadwood! Never have I experienced greater pleasure than was caused me by the announcement of the forthcoming arrival of this piano with which you honour me as a gift: I shall regard it as an Altar upon which I will give up the most beautiful offerings of my mind to the divine Apollo.'

1823 *Semiramide*, Rossini's last Italian opera, opens at Venice. The first act lasts 2½ hours.

1844 Berlioz conducts his *Roman Carnival* without rehearsal. 'To see Berlioz during [the first] performance was a sight never to be forgotten. He watched over every single member of the huge band, his beat was so decisive, his indication of all the nuances so clear and so unmistakable that the overture went smoothly' (Sir Charles Hallé).

1903 Priaulx Rainier, South Africa's only notable composer, is born in Natal. 'She never wrote two of anything.'[1]

[1]John Amis, obituary, the *Independent*, 15.10.86.

1715 'For fear of being maltreated and covered with spittle as on the previous occasion, we took a box, not very expensive, and had our revenge in behaving to the people below as people had to us ... The singers were incomparable' – a German architect revisits the San Angelo theatre in Venice, where Vivaldi is maestro.

1781 Josef Mysliveček, 43, noseless Bohemian composer – he lost the olfactory organ to advancing syphilis – succumbs to the disease in Rome. Known as 'il divino Boëmo', his melodic style influenced Mozart's.

1931 A piano concerto by Reynaldo Hahn, Proust's sometime lover, is played in Paris by Magda Tagliaferro. 'Reynaldo was a very great dandy. When he saw a musician who dressed shabbily or in poor taste, he would snort: "Amateur!"'[1]

[1]Tagliaferro NL.

1887 Verdi's *Otello* at La Scala. Two conductors play in the orchestra: Toscanini in the cellos and Tulio Serafin among the violins, who also number the grandfather and father of Sir John Barbirolli.

1907 Schoenberg's first string quartet is hissed in Vienna. When Mahler reproves a disrupter, he is told: 'I hiss your symphonies too!'

Schoenberg

1958 Broadcast live, Michael Tippett's Second symphony breaks down moments into its first performance. The conductor, Sir Adrian Boult, tells the audience 'Sorry, entirely my fault'; Tippett blames the first violin; the BBC holds the composer responsible.

1497 Johannes Ockeghem, luminous Flemish composer, dies at Tours, but so obscurely that he may have been any age from 67 to 87.

1813 Rossini's *Tancredi* at La Scala is abandoned in the middle of Act 2 when the leading ladies fall ill in each of the first two performances.

1851 Schumann's *Rhenish* symphony is applauded at Düsseldorf.

Debussy observed

1911 Debussy on Vienna: 'Raddled old city where one is surfeited with the music of Brahms and Puccini, with officers with women's bosoms and women with officers' chests.'

Vienna on Debussy: 'A broad-shouldered man with coal-black hair and pointed beard, slightly indolent and ponderous in his movements, with a somewhat sullen and weary glance.'

1786 Double premiere in the orangery at Schönbrunn Palace, Vienna: Mozart's *Der Schauspieldirektor* (*The Impresario*) immediately followed by *Prima la musica e poi la parole* (*First the music, then the words*) by his arch-rival, Salieri.

1928 'I was due to lunch with Charlie Chaplin but didn't think it would be much fun for either of us' – Ravel, in Hollywood.

1935 Fritz Kreisler, 60, admits composing a dozen pieces and passing them off as new-found works by Couperin, Dittersdorf, Porpora, Pugnani, Vivaldi and others. 'I found it impudent and tactless to repeat my [own] name endlessly on the programmes,' he explains.

1944 Lovely Lina Cavalieri, programme seller at Rome Opera, artiste at the Folies Bergère and star soprano at the Met and Covent Garden, dies in an Allied air raid as she ventures from a Florence shelter to rescue her jewels, worth $3,000,000.

1874 After twice being rejected by the censor, Mussorgsky stages a much-revised version of his masterpiece *Boris Godunov*.

1895 *The Black Mountain* by Augusta Holmès, who refused to marry Saint-Saëns but has three illegitimate children by the novelist Catulle Mendès, is staged at the Paris Opéra.

1904 Sibelius, 'red-faced and perspiring', conducts Viktor Nováček in 'a losing battle' with his violin concerto.

1908 Rachmaninov recovers confidence with his second symphony at St Petersburg. An anonymous admirer whom he never meets starts sending him white lilacs at every concert.

6 FEBRUARY

7 FEBRUARY

8 FEBRUARY

9 FEBRUARY

 **10 FEBRUARY**

 11 FEBRUARY

1885 Berg is born in Vienna and christened Alban Maria Johannes; the unusual first name is proposed by the Greek Consul.

1893 *Falstaff*, Verdi's last opera, opens at La Scala. 'Through all the excitement and triumph he remained what he is, a quiet, calm, modest gentleman; one of those intellectual giants who scorn to trade upon their greatness and are content to be as other men are.'[1]

1897 Debussy's first bout of domestic bother: 'Gaby, with her steely eyes, found in my pocket a letter that left no doubt about the advanced state of a love affair with romantic trimmings to move the hardest heart. So – tears, drama, a real revolver and a report in the *Petit Journal* ... It was all barbarous, useless and will change absolutely nothing.'

1967 Charlotte Moorman is arrested in New York for playing her cello topless; she receives, aptly enough, a suspended sentence.

[1]Sir Charles Stanford.

1881 Four months and five days after Offenbach's death, his masterpiece *Tales of Hoffmann* opens at the Opéra-Comique, where it is sung 101 times before the end of the year.

1927 Jazz and the Charleston invade opera in Krenek's *Jonny Spielt Auf* at Leipzig.

1948 The Central Committee of the Communist Party of the USSR, invoking Stalin's second bout of musical persecution, condemns 'comrades Shostakovich, Prokofiev, Khatchaturian, Shebalin, Popov, Myaskovsky and others for composing formalist perversions and anti-democratic tendencies alien to the Soviet people and its artistic tastes.' Prokofiev replies: 'No matter how painful it is for many composers, myself included, I agree to the resolution of the Central Committee which establishes the condition for making the whole organism of Soviet music healthy ... I have never doubted the importance of melody. I like melody very much ...'

1785 Joseph Haydn is initiated in Vienna as a Freemason. At a party given next day by his new lodge brother, Mozart, Haydn informs Leopold Mozart: 'I tell you before God and as an honest man, that your son is the greatest composer I know, either in person or by name.'

1840 Donizetti's first French opera, *La fille du régiment*, is an instant success. The second soprano, Marie Julie Boulanger, is grandmother of composers Nadia and Lili.

1843 Verdi's *I Lombardi alla Prima Crociata (The Lombards at the first crusade)* opens at La Scala, amid mutterings of sacrilege from the Archbishop of Milan. 'The humble people began to besiege the gallery as early as three o'clock so that the curtain rose to a strong odour of garlic sausages! There was no barrier to the success that was instantly proclaimed. The public wanted the quintet repeated but the police would not permit it ...'

1903 The Ninth Symphony that Bruckner was composing at the moment of his death is heard six years later in Vienna in a version cut and corrupted by an acolyte.

1797 Haydn's *Emperor Hymn* and new national anthem is sung in Vienna on the Kaiser's birthday. It is so catching that the Germans borrow the tune for their anthem, 'Deutschland, Deutschland über alles'.

1844 Rossini's *Cenerentola* is the first opera to be staged in Australia.

1894 Hans von Bülow, 64, influential conductor and pianist who invented 'the three Bs' for Bach, Beethoven and Brahms, dies while convalescing in Cairo. His Hamburg funeral gives Gustav Mahler the idea for the Totenfeier movement of his Second symphony.

1924 George Gershwin plays *Rhapsody in Blue* at the Aeolian Hall, New York, in a jazz concert staged by Paul Whiteman. 'It was snowing, but men and women were fighting to get into the door, pulling and mauling each other as they do sometimes at a baseball game, or a prize fight, or in the subway ... [The *Rhapsody*] is music conceived for the jazz orchestra, and I do not believe any other could do it justice ... My 23 boys that day played 36 instruments.'[1]

[1]Whiteman, in the *Saturday Evening Post*.

1741 Johann Joseph Fux, composer and pedant – his primer *Gradus ad Parnassum* is mocked by Debussy in *Children's Corner* – dies an octogenarian in Vienna and is buried with pomp inside St Stephen's.

1751 At the chorus 'How dark O Lord are thy decrees, all hid from mortal sight,' Handel breaks off his last oratorio, *Jephtha*, noting that he is 'unable to continue because the sight of my left eye is so weakened.'

1867 Johann Strauss II tries out *The Blue Danube* at a Fasching ball in Vienna. 'Not catching enough,' he decides.

1883 'Triste, triste, triste,' mourns Verdi, 'Wagner e morte.' At 3 p.m. Richard Wagner, 69, dies in Venice.

1813 Alexander Dargomyzhsky, pioneer of Russian opera with *Rusalka*, is born into a land-owning family in the Tula province and does not utter a sound until his sixth year.

1861 The first Italian Parliament assembles, with Verdi as an elected member.

Wagner mourned

1883 Cosima, who like Isolde hoped to die with her Tristan, is prised away from Wagner's corpse 30 hours after his demise. Before the coffin is closed, she cuts off all her hair and deposits it inside.

1969 Hans Werner Henze's *Essay on Pigs*, a reflection on police-student relations in West Berlin, is performed in London.

13 FEBRUARY

14 FEBRUARY

15 FEBRUARY

 16 FEBRUARY

 17 FEBRUARY

1857 Mikhail Ivanovich Glinka, 52, father of modern Russian music, perishes of a cold in Berlin. 'Glinka was a man of small character, and it is not surprising that his music is not marked by strong individual traits ...'. (David Brown/NG).

1927 Rumanian tenor Trajan Grozavescu, 33, rising star of Vienna opera, is shot dead by his jealous wife as he boards a train for a singing assignation in Berlin.

1947 Jascha Heifetz plays the D major violin concerto by ex-Viennese *wunderkind* Erich Wolfgang Korngold. 'More corn than gold,' grumbles a critic.

1829 François-Joseph Gossec, composer of the first French symphony, expires at Passy aged 95.

1848 Chopin, in his final Paris recital, too weak to attack a barcarolle with the required force, plays 'in the most opposite style, pianissimo, but with such wonderful nuances ...'

1892 Massenet's *Werther* is premiered in Vienna. 'Today *Werther* tomorrow *Thais* ... One work pushes aside another ... The great thing is to work constantly and to produce, and then to produce again ... You see, it is as Voltaire said: "We must cultivate our garden!"'[1]

1908 Gustav Mahler, leaning out of an eleventh-floor window of the Hotel Majestic, New York, weeps over the passing funeral procession of an heroic fire chief. The brief drum stroke of the cortège enters his Tenth symphony.

[1]Massenet, interviewed before the Paris premiere, 16 January 1893.

1870 Edvard Grieg, 26, in Rome, humbly calls on Liszt, who seizes his music portfolio and plays sight unseen the Violin and Piano Sonata, 'the whole thing, root and branch, violin and piano, nay more, for he played fuller, more broadly.'

1889 'The affirmation of incompetence pushed to dogmatic lengths,' declares Gounod loudly after César Franck's Symphony in D minor is played at the Paris Conservatoire.

1904 Puccini's *Madama Butterfly* at La Scala is destroyed by 'growls, shouts, groans and laughter' from the audience, culminating in hilarious cries of 'Butterfly is pregnant!' when Rosina Storchio's kimono billows out in front.

1917 'Twinkle, twinkle, little star' enters the concert repertoire in Ernst von Dohnanyi's *Variations on a Nursery Song* for piano and orchestra, played by the composer in Berlin.

1743 *Samson* brings down the house at Covent Garden. 'Handel has set up an Oratorio against the Operas, and succeeds.'

1869 Brahms' *German Requiem*, composed over 11 years and spurred to completion by his mother's death, is conducted at Leipzig by Carl Reinecke. Wagner calls it 'Schumann's last thought'; G. B. Shaw says the *Requiem* 'is patiently borne only by the corpse.'

Puccini fumes

1904 Puccini, undaunted, declares: 'My *Butterfly* remains as it is: the most heartfelt and expressive opera I have conceived. I shall win in the end, you'll see – given a smaller theatre less raddled with hatred and passion. Here I have withdrawn the opera and refunded the money.'

1843 A performance of *Norma* at the Royal Opera House, Madrid, is disrupted as the prima donna rushes off to give birth to a daughter. The infant becomes the diva Adelina Patti.

1910 Jules Massenet is enraptured at Monte Carlo by his own *Don Quichotte*, starring the mighty Russian bass, Chaliapin. 'Oh beautiful magnificent premiere!'

1934 George Gershwin gets his own radio show, sponsored by Feen-a-mint, a laxative.

1626 Who loves not Musicke and the heavenly muse, That man God hates. John Dowland, 63, melancholy melodist, is buried at Blackfriars.

1816 Rossini's *Barber of Seville*, titled *Almaviva* and composed in three weeks, is wrecked by fans of Paisiello's version of the Beaumarchais comedy. 'Coming out of the theatre by a secret door, I was recognised, unfortunately;

an angry mob with raised fists pursued me with such rage, ... that I thought the end of my existence had come ...' After the second performance Rossini is mobbed again – by newfound admirers.

1921 'I'd rather have written any symphony of Brahms' than any play of Ibsen's. I'd rather have written the first movement of Beethoven's *Eroica* than the *Song of Solomon*; it is not only far

more beautiful, it is also far more profound. A better man wrote it' – newspaper editor H. L. Mencken, to a literary critic.

1941 Rudolph Ganz plays his piano concerto on themes drawn from the number-plates of his two Ford automobiles (280893 in A minor, 501127 in A major), with Frederick Stock driving the Chicago Symphony Orchestra.

18 FEBRUARY

19 FEBRUARY

20 FEBRUARY

 **21 FEBRUARY**

 22 FEBRUARY

 23 FEBRUARY

1893 Andrés Segovia, reviver of the guitar as a classical instrument, is born in Granada. In his nineties he reflects: 'I have had three wives and three guitars, though I've flirted with others.'

1911 Marcel Proust, at home in bed, attends a performances of *Pelléas et Mélisande* at the Opéra-Comique through a 'theatrephone' pressed to his ear. He listens in regularly for several nights until he can sing the part of Pelléas.

1920 *Le Boeuf sur le Toit* (*The Bull on the Roof*), a satire by Darius Milhaud on US Prohibition laws, is danced at the Comédie des Champs-Elysées and adopted as the name of a Paris bistro.

1777 'At the last concert given by the Baron de Bagge, the two famous violinists Jarnovick and Pieltain quarrelled, accusing each other of playing out of tune. Pieltain struck Jarnovick, who leapt on the aggressor and scratched him with his fingernails; people tried to separate them; the defender having only his teeth free, used them to grab the end of Pieltain's nose ...'[1]

1888 Hugo Wolf to a friend: 'I have just put a new song on paper, a song for the gods.' Hours later: 'Hardly was my letter posted than I took up my Mörike and wrote another ... P.S. I have just succeeded in a third song, and *how!*'

1903 In a Vienna asylum, Wolf, 43, dies insane.

1940 Heitor Villa Lobos, between 5 and 6.40 p.m., traces a photograph of New York rooftops onto music paper and converts it into an engaging piano piece, *New York Skyline*.

[1]Métra, *Correspondance secrète*.

1685 Georg Friederich Händel – he anglicizes the name on becoming British – is born in Halle, Saxony, a barber-surgeon's son. 'From his very childhood, Handel had discovered such a strong propensity to Music that his father, who always intended him for the study of Civil Law, had reason to be alarmed ... [and] strictly forbad him to meddle with any musical instrument.'[1]

1835 *La Juive*, Halévy's martyred Jewish heroine, lays the foundations of French grand opera.

1881 Musorgsky, 41, declaring there is 'nothing left for him but to go and beg in the streets', has an alcoholic epileptic seizure and is rushed to hospital.

1897 Gustav Mahler to qualify for a post at the Vienna Opera, converts to Roman Catholicism.

1907 *Les Sylphides*, Fokine's ballet to Cho-

pin's music, is danced in St Petersburg.

1931 Dame Nellie Melba, 69, dies at Sydney.

1934 Shortly after 7.30 a.m. Sir Edward Elgar, 77, expires at Worcester.

Later that day, at a BBC rehearsal of *A Boy was Born*, Benjamin Britten makes the acquaintance of Peter Pears, his future lifelong companion.

[1]John Mainwaring.

1818 Dressed in formal English costume, 7-year-old Frédéric Chopin makes his debut at a charity concert playing a concerto by Gyrowetz. When asked what impressed the audience most, he replies: 'my collar'.

1823 Beethoven to King George IV of England: 'As long ago as 1813 the undersigned, complying with many requests from several Englishmen resident in Vienna, took the liberty of sending your Majesty his work entitled *Wellington's Battle* ... For many years the undersigned cherished the agreeable hope that Your Majesty would most graciously have him informed of the safe arrival of his work ...'

1848 I was just six years old ... 'We were at luncheon when the waitress rushed into the room like a maniac. *"Aux armes, citoyens!"* she yelled. I was too young to understand what was going on in the streets. All I can remember is that riots broke out and ... on the morning of that historic day, by the light of tallow candles (wax candles were only for the rich) my mother for the first time placed my fingers on the piano' – Jules Massenet.

1682 Alessandro Stradella, 39, having survived murder attempts by a Venetian grandee whose lady he had snatched, is stabbed to death while strolling in a Genoa piazza, apparently on the orders of his mistress, exasperated by the composer's chronic infidelities. His fate, much fancified, fuels four operas.

1881 Two of Fauré's *Trois romances sans paroles* are played in a Paris salon – music, muses Marcel Proust, 'that a pederast might hum while raping a choirboy.'

1906 Anton Arensky, 44, whose life – says his teacher Rimsky-Korsakov – 'ran a dissipated course between wine and card-playing, yet his activity as a composer was most fertile,' dies of consumption near St Petersburg.

1770 'He dreamed he had entered into a contract with the devil, in fulfilment of which his satanic majesty was bound to perform all his requests' – Guiseppe Tartini, composer of the *Devil's Trill* sonata, dies at Padua aged 78.

1852 Wagner meets his Zurich neighbours: 'A wealthy young merchant named Wesendonck ... his wife is very pretty and seems to have developed a crush on me ... True, I can no longer enjoy the company of men, or even of women; but the latter are the last element that still now and then creates some slight illusion for me.' Mathilde Wesendonck becomes his mistress and inspires *Tristan and Isolde.*

1879 Frank Bridge, best remembered for variations on one of his themes by his pupil Benjamin Britten, is born in Brighton.

1943 On the Red Army's 25th anniversary, US composer Roy Harris is 'proud to dedicate my Fifth symphony to the heroic and freedom-loving people of our great ally, the USSR.'

24 FEBRUARY

25 FEBRUARY

26 FEBRUARY

27 FEBRUARY

 28 FEBRUARY

29 FEBRUARY

1854 Schumann, 43, throws himself off a bridge into the Rhine; he is rescued by four boatmen and tries to jump back in. 'Schumann's nerves ... worsened from day to day; he heard music continuously, sometimes it was most beautiful but often agonizingly hideous.'

1873 Enrico Caruso is born in Naples.

Sad Schumann

1887 Chatting animatedly with friends around midnight at a St Petersburg ball, Borodin staggers suddenly and falls down dead. He is 53.

1901 The remains of Giuseppe and Giuseppina Verdi are escorted to their final resting place at the Home for Musicians they founded in Milan. 28,000 people follow the cortège singing, softly, 'Va, pensiero' from *Nabucco*.

1847 Berlioz reaches Russia. 'From what I had heard of the strictness of the Imperial Police, I expected to have my rolls of music confiscated for at least a week ...'

1877 At lunch Wagner startles his wife with the complete *Parsifal* in prose dialogue. 'In the afternoon I read it by myself. This is bliss, this is solace, this is sublimity and devotion!!' (CWD).

1912 Carl Nielsen conducts his *Sinfonia espansiva* and violin concerto, with his son-in-law, Emil Telmányi, as soloist.

1920 Ravel's *Tombeau de Couperin* is performed, his tribute 'not so much to an individual as to the whole of French music of the 18th century.'

1975 Sir Neville Cardus, low-born Mancunian and the only music critic to be knighted (most probably for his cricket writing), signs off aged 85.

1792 The reason for his eternal youthfulness, says Gioacchino Rossini, is that his birthday falls but once in four years. 'The Swan of Pesaro' enters the world on the extra day of a leap year.

1836 Giacomo Meyerbeer's five-act, no-expense-spared *Les Huguenots* resounds in Paris and throughout the 19th century. Mazzini, the Italian liberator, reports: 'In a transitional time like ours we cannot expect the high priest of the music of the future to appear among us; Meyerbeer, however, is the forerunner sent to announce his coming.'

1892 Richard Strauss conducts his *Macbeth* symphonic poem in Berlin. At rehearsal Hans von Bülow admonishes him: 'You should have the score in your head, not your head in the score!'

M * A * R * C * H

1875 After the dress rehearsal of *Carmen*, 'everyone, from the director of the theatre to the concierge turned his back on Bizet.'

1906 'You know I'm not a bit jealous; the real sea plays with the waves even better than I do ...' Debussy, composer of *La Mer* to his publisher.

1919 On Richard Strauss's arrival as director of the Vienna State Opera, most of the 800 employees walk out, complaining that his salary is too high 'for an impoverished nation like the new Austria' and that his own operas will be performed too much.

1925 *Intégrales*, a work for wind and percussion by Edgar Varese with electronic premonitions, is conducted in New York by Leopold Stokowski. 'The title of a score is of no importance,' warns the composer.

1795 Haydn in London performs his penultimate symphony, the *Drumroll*.

1884 Delius sails from Liverpool to run an orange grove in Florida.

1900 Kurt Weill is born in Dessau, son of the synagogue cantor.

1923 *Joseph, oh Joseph, why are you so chaste?'* is the hit song in Leo Fall's *Madame Pompadour* in Vienna.

1924 Sibelius concludes his Seventh symphony, Op. 105: his 33 remaining years are silent.

Haydn in rolls

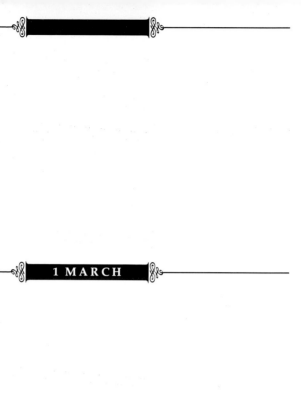

1 MARCH

2 MARCH

1860 Brahms' first serenade is heard at Hanover. 'A monstrosity, a caricature, a freak, which should never have been published much less performed *here* ... it is inexcusable that such filth should have been offered to a public thirsting for good music. That was an hour – a fiendish torture that can never be forgotten. Poor Mozart, poor Beethoven!' (anonymous letter to Brahms' friend, Joseph Joachim).

Early Brahms

1875 *Carmen* flops. 'After the fourth act, which was glacial from start to finish, no one [applauded] except three or four faithful and sincere friends of Bizet's. They had reassuring phrases on their lips, but sadness in their eyes.'

1932 Eugen D'Albert, 67, composer of 19 operas and husband of 6 wives, expires in Riga while working on the 20th, *Mr Wu*, and seeking a divorce.

1678 Antonio Vivaldi is born in the midst of a Venetian earthquake and baptised immediately by the midwife for fear he might perish.

1791 'ANNOUNCEMENT Herr Bähr, chamber musician presently in the service of his Imperial Russian Majesty, will have the honour of being heard playing several pieces on the clarinet at a grand musical concert ... in Herr Jahn's hall; Mme Lange will sing and Herr Kapellmeister Mozart will play a concerto on the pianoforte' – it is Mozart's last solo performance, playing the 27th piano concerto, K595.

1798 Giovanni Battista Viotti, legendary violinist, is expelled from Britain on charges of revolutionary agitation trumped up by jealous musicians.

1869 'Beethoven's grand-nephew has come begging again,' notes Cosima Wagner.

1877 *Swan Lake* is danced in Moscow.

1778 Thomas Arne, 67, composer of 'Rule, Britannia!' expires at 8 p.m. 'I was talking on the subject of music with the Doctor ... when, in attempting to illustrate what he had advanced, he in a very feeble and tremulous voice sung part of an air, during which he became progressively more faint until he breathed his last, making as our immortal Shakespeare expresses it, a swan-like end fading in music' (Joseph Vernon, tenor).

1887 Heitor Villa-Lobos – 'I learnt music from a bird in the jungles of Brazil, not from academies' – is born in Rio de Janeiro.

1905 At the dot of 6 p.m. Debussy finishes *La Mer*.

1942 Shostakovich's Seventh symphony, named after his native Leningrad and composed during its siege, is played at Kuibyshev on the Volga by the evacuated Bolshoi orchestra under Samuel Samosud. 'It's not about

Leningrad under siege, it's about the Leningrad that Stalin destroyed and Hitler merely finished off' (Shostakovich, to Solomon Volkov).

1953 Three hours before his tormentor Stalin's death, Sergei Prokofiev, 61, suffers a fatal brain haemorrhage.

1831 The sleepwalking opera, Bellini's *La Sonnambula*, opens in Milan.

1853 Verdi to his publisher: 'I am sorry that I must give you sad news but I cannot conceal the truth from you. *La Traviata* was a failure. Let us not investigate the reasons. That is what happened. Farewell, farewell.'

1913 The term 'jazz' is coined by Scoop Gleeson in a San Francisco newspaper article reporting the return of a baseball team: 'Everybody has come back to the old town, full of the old "jazz" and they promise to knock the fans off their feet ...'

1932 On his way to give a concert at Reading, Pennsylvania, bandmaster John Philip Sousa dies aged 77. 'The Stars and Stripes Forever', composed in 1897, has earned him more than $300,000.

1786 Franz Benda, founder of a Bohemian musical dynasty and leader of Frederick the Great's orchestra in more than 10,000 concerts in which the King plays flute solos, dies aged 78 near Potsdam.

1821 Schubert's *Erlkönig* is sung by his friend Michael Vogl at a public concert in Vienna, creating a tremendous impression.

1875 Maurice Ravel is born at Ciboure on the Basque coast. His father, a mechanic, is absent in Paris, seeking employment.

1928 Asked what he wants for his 53rd birthday, Ravel says: to meet Gershwin. 'George that night surpassed himself, achieving astounding feats in rhythmic intricacies; even Ravel was dumbfounded' (Eva Gauthier).

1869 Hector Berlioz, 65, dies alone in his Paris apartment on rue de Calais. 'My contempt for the folly and baseness of mankind, my hatred of its atrocious cruelty, have never been so intense. And I say hourly to Death: "When you will." What is he waiting for?'

1902 Sibelius in Helsingfors conducts his second, sunniest symphony, dreamed up in Italy.

1920 Muzak is conceived at the Galéries Barbazange when, between the acts of a Max Jacob play, Erik Satie presents *musique d'ameublement* ('furniture music'): to be heard but not listened to. 'It was no use for Satie to shout: "Go on talking! Walk about! Don't listen!" They listened without speaking. The whole effect was spoilt. Satie had not bargained for the charm of his own music' (Milhaud, *Notes Without Music*).

1983 Sir William Walton, British composer, bows out aged 80 on the island of Ischia, where he chose self-exile.

1984 'Stop the idiotic ratings game,' implores composer Peter Maxwell Davies at a European broadcasters' conference on music on television. 'Pop music is in its death throes,' adds his junior colleague, Nigel Osborne.

6 MARCH

 7 MARCH

 8 MARCH

1842 Verdi, 28, conquers La Scala with *Nabucco*; its Hebrew slaves' chorus *'Va, pensiero'* is perceived by Italians as a proclamation of their liberty.

1844 *Ernani* at Venice marks 'the coronation of Verdi as first composer of the world.'

1849 Otto Nicolai's *Merry Wives of Windsor*, rejected by Vienna, triumphs in Berlin.

1902 Gustav Mahler, 41, director of the Vienna Court Opera and a confirmed bachelor, is seduced into marriage by Alma Schindler, a 22-year-old would-be composer.

Verdi triumphant

1749 Lorenzo da Ponte, Mozart's librettist, is born Emanuele Conigliano in the Jewish ghetto at Ceneda, northern Italy. He is baptised at 14, takes the name of the bishop of Ceneda and becomes a priest.

1870 Arch-conservative Ignaz Moscheles – 'I find Chopin's productions on the whole too sugared, too little worthy of a man and an educated musician' – dies aged 75 in Leipzig where he is professor of piano.

1910 His successor, Carl Reinecke, teacher of Grieg, Sullivan and Albeniz and himself a prolific composer, dies there aged 85.

1936 When George Enescu's *Oedipe* is staged at the Paris Opéra, the Rumanian composer-violinist smashes his priceless Guarnerius during rehearsals in a fit of sexual jealousy.

1829 A century after it was last heard, the *St Matthew Passion* is directed in Berlin by the 20-year-old Felix Mendelssohn, inaugurating the Bach revival.

1851 Venice acclaims Verdi and *Rigoletto*.

1867 His *Don Carlos* is savagely cut in Paris.

Verdi reclines

1876 US composer Carl Ruggles (*Men and Mountains*) is born at East Marion, Massachusetts.

1903 Ethel Smyth's *Der Wald* is the only opera by a woman ever to be seen at the Met.

604 Saint Gregory dies. His name is given to the liturgical chant of the Roman church.

1857 Verdi's *Simon Boccanegra* opens in Venice, 'a fiasco almost as great as that of *Traviata*.'

1912 Henry Cowell, 15, demonstrates his 'tone clusters' at the San Francisco Music Club, banging his fists and forearms on its keyboard.

1936 'Schoenberg, in my judgement, is more of a chemist of music than an artistic creator' – Stravinsky, interview in *La Noche*, Barcelona.

1945 In the final Allied advance, the Vienna Opera House is bombed. Six weeks later, opera resumes with *Figaro* at the Volksoper.

1628 John Bull, probable composer of 'God Save the King', dies in Antwerp aged 75. He fled England on charges of lewdness, the Archbishop of Canterbury having complained that 'Bull is as famous for marring of virginity as he is for fingering of organs and virginals.'

1833 Mendelssohn finishes his Italian Symphony and sends the score to London for copying and rehearsal. For two years' exclusive rights, he is paid £100 by the Philharmonic Society.

1861 The Paris version of Wagner's *Tannhäuser*, sung in French and with an Act 2 ballet, turns into a famous fiasco as young aristocrats of the Jockey Club loudly parade their xenophobia. Wagner calls off the farce after three performances. 'The one success of the opera was the appearance of the sporting dogs which the Emperor had specially lent from the Royal kennels.'

1860 After tootling his piccolo from the roof of a cab in the rue Montmartre, flamboyant conductor Louis Jullien, 47, suffers a fatal haemorrhage in the lunatic asylum to which he has been escorted.

1885 *The Mikado* by Gilbert and Sullivan opens at the Savoy and runs for almost two years despite petitions by the Japanese ambassador to have it suppressed on grounds of racial offensiveness and sadism.

'I seized him by his little pig-tail,
And on his knees fell he,
As he squirmed and struggled,
And gurgled and guggled,
I drew my snickersee!
Oh never shall I
Forget the cry,
Or the shriek that shrieked he ...'

1941 'Gustav Mahler is to Richard Strauss as Bach to Handel, or Debussy to Ravel ...' – critical aphorism by Virgil Thomson.

12 MARCH

 13 MARCH

 14 MARCH

15 MARCH

 16 MARCH

 17 MARCH

1842 Luigi Cherubini's passing is eased by knowing that he has composed for himself a superb D minor *Requiem*, with male voices alone to render it acceptable in church. As head of the Paris Conservatoire, the 82-year-old Italian has blocked musical progress for two decades.

1918 Lili Boulanger, 24, the first woman composer to win the Prix de Rome, dies in Paris of intestinal tuberculosis endured since infancy.

1956 *My Fair Lady* opens on Broadway.

1981 *Donnerstag*, the first of Stockhausen's projected seven-day *Licht* cycle of operas, opens in Milan, depicting the hero Michael's sexual and artistic arousal, trans-global voyage and homecoming, and ending with a *Donnerstag-Abschied* fanfare blown by five trumpeters standing on roofs outside the theatre. Striking technicians, however, abort the grand finale.

1736 Pergolesi, 26, depressed at the failure of his operas, dies while writing a Stabat Mater. 'He had no sooner ceased to live than he became the object of an interest only equal to the indifference shown him in his lifetime.'

1833 Bellini's *Beatrice di Tenda* opens in Venice amid orchestrated opposition. It was so hissed that, whilst singing the great duet [Giuditta] Pasta stepped forward and, with a grand, significant gesture, addressed to the public the words, 'Se amar non puoi, rispettami! (If you cannot love, respect me).' The immense applause that ensued allowed that exquisite opera to be heard to its end.

1840 Schumann hears Liszt play at Leipzig: 'In a matter of seconds we have been exposed to tenderness, daring, fragrance, and madness.'

1792 Haydn is bled in London.

1830 Chopin plays his F minor concerto in Warsaw.

1843 The chorus 'Down with tyrants! Never, never will the English rule in France!' in Halévy's opera *Charles VI* provokes audience demonstrations against the prevailing entente in Anglo-French relations.

1872 Wagner wearies of composing. At the arrival of Siegfried's corpse, he writes in the score, 'see *Tristan* Act III.'

1844 Nikolay Rimsky-Korsakov is born at Tikhvin. 'Our house stood almost at the end of the town, on the bank of the Tikhvina River, on the other bank of which, opposite us, was situated the Tikhvin Monastery.'

1902 Enrico Caruso, 29, is lured into a room at the Hotel di Milano by a £100 offer from record producer Fred Gaisberg. The ten arias that he bellows into the waiting horn prove to be the first acceptable recordings of the singing voice, Caruso's volume and timbre overcoming the ineradicable crackle of surface noise.

1927 At a Berlin radio rehearsal, Bertolt Brecht meets Kurt Weill.

1927 Rachmaninov plays his Fourth Concerto in Philadelphia but withdraws it for revision. Critics spot a resemblance between the slow movement theme and the nursery rhyme, 'Three Blind Mice'.

1823 Beethoven delivers the *Missa Solemnis* to Archduke Rudolph.

1859 Gounod's *Faust* opens coolly at the Théâtre Lyrique. One critic states that it will not replace Spohr's opera on the same subject.

1896 Dvořák's cello concerto is premiered in London. Brahms, on seeing the score, exclaims: 'Why on earth did I not know that one could write a cello concerto like this? If only I had known, I'd have written one years ago!'

1955 For the second time in his life conductor Erich Kleiber flees the Berlin State Opera, first escaping the Nazis, now complaining that the Communists are subjugating art to propaganda.

1768 Boccherini, 25, makes his Paris debut playing a cello sonata. 'His notes struck the ear as harsh, his chords as unharmonious' (*Le Mercure de France*).

1812 Jan Ladislav Dussek, 52, Czech pianist and composer in the service of the French statesman Talleyrand, succumbs to gluttony and alcoholism. 'The extraordinary sensation he produced is not forgotten. Until then the pianoforte had only been heard to disadvantage as a concert instrument but under the hands of Dussek it eclipsed all that surrounded it' (F-J. Fétis).

1866 Rikard Nordraak, 24, composer of Norway's national anthem 'Yes, we love this land' to words by his cousin B. M. Bjørnson, dies of consumption in Berlin where he has been abandoned by his travelling companion, Grieg. The latter, grief-stricken, declares: 'His cause shall be my cause, his goal mine.'

18 MARCH

19 MARCH

20 MARCH

22 MARCH

1685 At Eisenach in the central German province of Thuringia, an eighth and last child is born to court musician Johann Ambrosius Bach. He is named Johann Sebastian.

1707 'Nothing is capable of being well set to music that is not nonsense' – Joseph Addison on opera.

1839 Modest Petrovich Musorgsky, Russia's most imaginative composer, is born into a landed, serf-owning household at Karevo, Pskov district. 'Musorgsky cannot be classed with any existing group of musicians ... His view, as a composer, of the task of art: art is a means of communication with people, not an aim in itself.' (Self-assessment).

1839 More than a decade after Schubert's death, and at Schumann's urging, Mendelssohn performs the Great C major Symphony in Leipzig.

1884 Dvořák to his dad: 'Who could have thought that far across the sea, in this enormous London, I should one day celebrate triumphs such as few foreign artists have known! ... If all the Czechs in Bohemia were put together, they would not equal the number of people living in London. And if all the inhabitants of the town of Kladno were to visit the enormous hall where I conducted my *Stabat Mater*, there would still be plenty of room – for that is how huge the Albert Hall is!'

1904 In New York, Richard Strauss conducts his *Symphonia Domestica*, depicting 24 hours with his family – 'either a deplorable aberration of taste or else a clever method of courting publicity' (*New York Evening Post*). 'I see no reason why I should not write a symphony about myself. I find the subject as interesting as Napoleon or Alexander the Great,' retorts the composer.

1907 'MUST IMMEDIATELY LEAVE AMERICA PLEASE CABLE ME 600 RUBLES' Alexander Scriabin wires Glazunov for help after US newsmen discover that the woman travelling with him is not Mrs Scriabin.

1925 Ravel's opera, *L'enfant et les sortilèges*, libretto by Colette, opens at Monte Carlo. 'He seemed concerned only with the "duo miaouw" between the two Cats and asked me gravely if I saw any problem in replacing the "mouao" by "mouain"' (Colette: *Looking Backwards*).

1936 Alexander Glazunov, 71, once hailed as 'little Glinka', dies in Parisian exile. His body is returned 36 years later to Leningrad.

1619 'Saturday never comes but I sigh to see it here so soon' – Monteverdi, overworked in Venice.

1687 Jean-Baptiste Lully, 55, dies of a self-inflicted conductor's injury (see 8 Jan), receiving Christian absolution for his dissolute life after pretending to burn his remaining opera-ballets.

Hirsute Roussel

1908 Albert Roussel's First symphony, *Poem of the Forest*, is heard in Brussels.

1951 William Mengelberg, 79, conductor for half a century of Amsterdam's Concertgebouw orchestra, dies in Switzerland, having been banned for life from Dutch music for cultural collaboration with the Nazi occupiers.

1703 Vivaldi, 25, enters the priesthood. He soon gives up saying Mass, claiming that a respiratory illness keeps forcing him to leave the altar in mid-devotion; others allege that he dashes to the sacristy to jot down musical themes.

1792 Haydn springs his 'Surprise' symphony. 'Was it true that he wrote the *Andante* with the kettle-drum bang to awaken the English who had fallen asleep in his concert? "No", he replied, "I wanted to surprise the public with something new and ... not to be outdone by my pupil Pleyel whose concerts had begun eight days before mine".'

1806 'A martyr to dissipation', George Frederick Pinto, composer of three remarkably advanced piano sonatas, dies in London aged 20.

1808 Maria Malibran, Spanish mezzo tragedienne, utters her first cry. 'As a child I often used to cry during my singing lessons. I did not want my father to notice it so I used to stand behind him and learned to get full control of my voice while my tears were flowing.'

1865 Dvořák, 23, finishes his First Symphony, *The Bells of Zlonice.* 'When my father came to live at Zlonice in 1856 he taught me his trade, and I learned how to buy sheep and kill them. But I liked my musical studies better' – interview in the *Sunday Times.*

1916 In broad daylight, in the English Channel between Folkestone and Dieppe, neutral Spanish composer Enrique Granados, 48, is drowned when a German submarine sinks the SS *Sussex.*

1984 *Akhnaten*, ancient Egyptian opera by Philip Glass, opens at Stuttgart.

1436 At the dedication of Florence Cathedral by Pope Eugenius IV with a motet by Dufay, 'the whole space of the church was filled with such choruses of harmony and such a concord of diverse instruments that it seemed (not without reason) as though the symphonies and songs of the angels and of divine paradise had been sent forth from the heavens to whisper in our ears an unbelievable celestial sweetness.'

1746 Gluck gives a concert in London with Handel, who says of him, 'he knows no more of counterpoint than my cook, Waltz.'

1867 Arturo Toscanini enters the world at Parma.

1881 Béla Bartók is born at Nagyszentmiklós.

1918 Too weak to be taken to the cellar during a long-range bombardment, Claude Debussy dies in his Paris home, aged 55, of rectal cancer. '*Il est mort, Claude de France,*' mourns the Italian poet, d'Annunzio.

1918 Karl Muck, German conductor of the Boston Symphony Orchestra, is arrested as an enemy alien and interned at Fort Oglethorpe, Georgia.

 **23 MARCH**

 **24 MARCH**

 **25 MARCH**

26 MARCH

 27 MARCH

 28 MARCH

1778 Beethoven, aged 7, gives his first concert: 'various clavier concertos and trios in which he flatters himself that he will give complete enjoyment to all ladies and gentlemen.'

1827 'At [the] startling, awful peal of thunder, the dying man suddenly raised his head . . . stretched out his right arm majestically – "like a General giving orders to an army" – the arm sunk back; he fell back; Beethoven was dead' (A. W. Thayer, *Life of Beethoven*).

1925 Pierre Boulez, musical iconoclast – 'Anyone who has not felt the necessity of the 12-tone language is superfluous' – is born at Montbrison in the Loire.

1973 In Jamaica, where only 'Mad dogs and Englishmen/Go out in the midday sun', composer and songwriter Sir Noël Coward, 73, shuts his eyes.

1416 Antonio Squarcialupi, organist of Florence Cathedral, licensed butcher and composer, is born. None of his own music survives, but his manuscript library, the Squarcialupi Codex, is a major source of 14th-century music.

1783 'Wolfgang Amadé Mozart takes pity on Leutgeb, ass, ox and simpleton . . .' reads the dedication of the horn concerto K417 to Joseph Leutgeb, whom Mozart makes crawl on all fours to retrieve the pages he cruelly scatters.

1897 Rachmaninov's First Symphony is calamitously conducted by Alexander Glazunov. The distraught composer wants to destroy the score, but is persuaded merely to suppress it. César Cui declares: 'If there were a conservatory in Hell, if one of its students were ordered to write a symphony on the Plagues of Egypt, and if he were to compose one like Mr Rachmaninov's, he would have succeeded brilliantly and delighted the inhabitants of Hell.'

1842 Members of the Imperial Court Orchestra give their first concert as the Vienna Philharmonic; the conductor is Otto Nicolai.

1881 At 5 a.m. crying, 'It's the end! Woe is me!', Modest Mussorgsky expires in a St Petersburg hospital after consuming an illicit bottle of brandy. He is 42.

1910 Manchester, says its *Guardian* newspaper, is better suited to concert than opera as its dull climate and murky atmosphere are 'unfavourable to a refined sense of visual form and colour.'

1937 'J'ai froid, j'ai froid,' murmurs Karol Szymanowski, Polish composer, dying at 55 in a Swiss sanatorium.

1943 Three days short of his 70th birthday, Sergei Rachmaninov is claimed in Los Angeles by cancer.

1827 An old woman watching Beethoven's funeral procession mutters, 'They're burying the general of the musicians.' Franz Grillparzer, in his graveside eulogy, says: 'He withdrew from mankind after he had given them his all and received nothing in return.'

1871 Queen Victoria opens the Royal Albert Hall in memory of her departed consort, one of whose compositions is played on the occasion.

1879 Tchaikovsky's *Eugene Onegin* is staged indifferently in Moscow. Nikolay Rubinstein likes it; his brother, Anton, loathes it.

1888 Charles-Valentin Alkan, 74, reclusive French composer, is found 'crushed beneath his upturned bookcase, from which he had been extracting a Hebrew religious book.'

1862 Balakirev, 25, founds the Free School of Music in St Petersburg to educate needy musicians and integrate Russian music with Western.

1865 'I myself play hardly anything but Beethoven' – Hermann von Helmholtz, founder of the science of musical acoustics, to a colleague.

1936 Conchita Supervia, internationally adored Spanish mezzo, is killed at 40 by childbirth complications.

1941 Britten's *Sinfonia da Requiem*, intended for the 2600th anniversary of the Japanese ruling dynasty, is spurned in Tokyo for its Christian sentiments and performed instead in New York.

1824 'I am the unhappiest, wretchedest creature in the world. Picture a man whose health will never entirely recover and who in his despair about it makes matters worse ... every night I go to bed hoping I shall not wake again, each morning only brings back the grief of the day before' – Schubert, 27, tormented by syphilis.

1837 Liszt and Thalberg, pianistic potentates, confront one another at the keyboard in a Paris salon. Their hostess adjudicates: 'Thalberg is the first pianist in the world; Liszt is the only one.'

1841 At Leipzig, Schumann's First is 'received with a sympathy that I think has not been given to any modern symphony since Beethoven,' he reports.

1913 A Vienna concert of works by Schoenberg and his associates is abandoned after violent disturbances resulting in several arrests. 'I should have brought my revolver,' mutters Schoenberg.

 **29 MARCH**

 30 MARCH

 31 MARCH

 1 APRIL

 2 APRIL

A · P · R · I · L

1831 Berlioz, determined to murder his faithless fiancée, Camille Moke, leaves Rome for home but thinks twice at Nice.

1901 'On Sundays, when God is kind, I shall hear no music.' Debussy begins his career as a critic.

Weary Cosima

1917 Scott Joplin, 49, ragtime composer, dies syphilitically insane at the Manhattan State Hospital.

1930 Cosima Wagner, 92, fades away at Bayreuth, having outlasted her Richard by 47 years.

1842 A Philharmonic Society is formed in New York by Urieli Corelli Hill. As the New York Philharmonic Orchestra, its inaugural concert is held on December 7.

1975 Pierre Boulez conducts his haunting *Rituel in memoriam Bruno Maderna*, for his late friend and fellow-composer.

1951 In the middle of the Grieg concerto at Carnegie Hall, the pianist, Simon Barere, falls down dead.

1973 'One of the greatest regrets in dying is that I shall never again be able to hear [Mahler's] *Das Lied von der Erde*,' mourns conductor Jascha Horenstein, 73.

1607 'The swan, they say, when his death is near, sings more sweetly' writes William Byrd, 64, in his *Gradualia*.

1711 'This inclination of the [Paris opera] audience to sing along with the actors so prevails with them that I have sometimes known the performers on the stage do no more in a celebrated song than the clerk of a parish church, who serves only to raise the psalm and is afterwards drowned in the music of the congregation' – Joseph Addison.

1832 Liszt and Chopin share a Paris concert platform.

1897 At 8.30 a.m. in his Vienna apartment, Johannes Brahms dies, aged 63, of cancer of the liver.

1787 'As death, when we come to consider it closely, is the true goal of our existence, I have formed during the last few years such close relations with this best and truest friend of mankind that his image not only terrifies me no longer but is in fact very soothing and consoling! And I thank my God for graciously granting me the opportunity (you understand my meaning) of learning that death is the key which unlocks the door to our true happiness. I never lie down at night without reflecting that – young as I am – I may not live to see another day' – Mozart to his dying father.

1877 A New York audience at Steinway Hall hears Frederic Boskovitz play a piano solo in Philadelphia – through Alexander Graham Bell's newly invented telephone.

1943 Raoul Laparra, 66, composer of the opera *La Habanera* and music critic of *Le Matin,* is killed in an Allied air raid on Suresnes, near Paris.

1954 Toscanini's last NBC broadcast is abandoned when the 87-year-old maestro gets miserably lost in the *Tannhäuser* overture; a recording of Brahms' First Symphony is substituted.

1874 *Die Fledermaus* takes wing in Vienna once Johann Strauss and his librettist have agreed to remove the line: 'In my palais, every lady may dress or undress as she pleases.'

1908 Herbert von Karajan, by far the most recorded conductor in history, is born in Salzburg. 'The composer manipulates from the moment he lifts up his pen. The concert hall manipulates because each seat is different ... And my manipulation as a conductor is that I try to bring out the sound I want. That is my handwriting' (interview in *The Times*, 12.10.77).

1946 A belated performance of Charles Ives' Third symphony wins him the Pulitzer Prize. 'Prizes are for boys,' snaps the 72-year-old composer. 'I'm grown up.'

1967 Weeks after his annual New York recital, fabled fiddler Mischa Elman dies in his 77th year. 'You know, the critics never change; I am still getting the same notices I used to get as a child. They tell me I play very well for my age.'

3 APRIL

 4 APRIL

 5 APRIL

7 APRIL

8 APRIL

1856 Borodin is engaged as a surgeon at a Tsarist military hospital. 'One day they brought in six serfs who had been flogged for shutting Colonel V. in the stables. Borodin had to pull the splinters from their backs. He fainted three times at the sight of the skin hanging in tatters ...'

1897 On the day of Brahms' funeral, Gustav Mahler is named Kapellmeister at the Vienna Court Opera.

1929 A Soviet electrical engineer in Tomsk names his newborn son after the inventor of light-bulbs: Edison Denisov becomes a composer in electronic and other media.

1971 Igor Stravinsky, 88, dies in his New York apartment at 5.20 a.m.

1724 Bach's *St John Passion* is sung on Good Friday at Leipzig.

1787 Beethoven, 17, arrives in Vienna and is taken to play to Mozart who declares: 'Keep your eyes on him; some day he will give the world something to talk about.'

1805 As the *Eroica* symphony is being performed at the Theater an der Wien, a man in the gallery calls out, 'I'll give a kreutzer if the thing will only stop.'

1829 'Napoleon', reflects Goethe, 'managed the world as [J. N.] Hummel his piano; both achievements appear wonderful, we do not understand one more than the other.'

1968 A 15-year-old schoolboy, Oliver Knussen, directs the London Symphony Orchestra in his First symphony; Knussen's father is the orchestra's principal double-bass player.

1692 Giuseppe Tartini, famed violinist, bows in at Pirano and at 21 elopes with a member of the Cardinal's household. 'He married early a wife of the Xantippe sort, and his patience upon the most trying occasions was always truly Socratic' (Burney, *Travels*).

1835 'As the closing strains began, I saw Liszt's countenance assume that agony of expression, mingled with radiant smiles of joy, which I never saw in any human face except in the paintings of our Saviour ... his hands rushed over the keys, the floor on which I sat shook like a wire and the whole audience were wrapped in sound when the hand and frame of the artist gave way; he fainted ...' – concert in Paris.

1848 Donizetti, 50 and insane, dies in his native Bergamo.

1851 Verdi, to his librettist: 'Dear Cammarano, I have read your sketch. As a gifted and very superior man you will not be offended if I humbly take the liberty of telling you that it's better to give up [*Trovatore*], if we cannot treat it with the boldness and novelty of the Spanish drama ...'

1889 'Drunkenness in private,' notes Tchaikovsky in his diary.

Tchaikovsky, sober

1916 *Nights in the Garden of Spain* is lamely performed in Madrid by the composer's pianist friend José Cubiles. In the audience is Arthur Rubinstein, who immediately adopts De Falla's quasi-concerto.

1935 Aulis Sallinen, Finland's foremost living composer, is born at Salmi.

1782 Dictionarist Denis Diderot begs the composer François-André Philidor to give up playing simultaneous blindfold chess matches in London cafés, where he is uncrowned world champion. 'I could forgive these dangerous experiments if you wagered enough to win five or six hundred guineas. But to risk your talent and your reason for nothing is simply inconceivable. To risk going mad for vanity's sake is stupid. When you have lost your [musical] talent, will the English step in to rescue your family?'

1853 *Ave Maria*, a 'mischievous prank' perpetrated by Charles Gounod on Bach's first prelude and a pious prayer, is played in Paris.

1906 At the Teatro San Carlo in Naples, the career of *Tess*, Frédéric d'Erlanger's opera after Thomas Hardy, is cut abruptly short by the eruption of Vesuvius.

1199 Richard I, warrior king of England and spare-time composer – his song, 'Yes, No Prisoner Can Tell His Story', survives – dies in France, of gangrene sustained from an arrow wound.

1727 *'Eli, Eli, lama sabathani'* – Christ's last words on the Cross – crown Bach's *St Matthew Passion*, sung at St Thomas's Church, Leipzig.

1814 The first performance of the *Archduke* trio is Beethoven's last as a pianist. 'The piano was badly out of tune, which Beethoven minded little since he did not hear it ... there was scarcely anything left of [his] virtuosity' (Spohr).

1947 'Shostakovich is a hard worker. His day begins at 7.30 a.m. when he and his two children – Galina, aged 11, and Maxim, aged 9 – do their physical jerks together to the accompaniment of the radio. The composer, by the way, is quite a sports fan. Football is his passion. Until noon he works at home answering his mail ... On the days when he is not due at the Conservatory he usually listens to music by composers who submit their work to the Stalin Prize committee ...' (*Moscow News*).

9 APRIL

10 APRIL

11 APRIL

13 APRIL

1722 Pietro Nardini, Tartini's successor, bows in at Livorno. 'Nardini is a violinist of love ... One has seen ice-cold aristocrats cry when he played an Adagio. He himself would shed tears, which fell on his violin' (Daniel Schubart).

1938 Feodor Chaliapin, 65, mighty Russian bass, dies in Paris of diabetic complications. Rachmaninov mourns: 'Chaliapin will never die.' *Izvestia* comments: 'Chaliapin betrayed his fatherland and sold his people for petty cash.'

1945 As Germany is overrun by Allied forces, the Berlin Philharmonic broadcasts Bruckner's Fourth and Richard Strauss completes *Metamorphosen* for 23 string instruments.

1961 A song by Shostakovich – 'My homeland hears, my homeland knows, where in the skies her son soars on' – is declaimed by cosmonaut Yuri Gagarin as he thankfully re-enters earth's orbit.

1377 Guillaume de Machaut, 'master of all melody', dies at Rheims in his eighth decade.

1627 The very first German opera, *Dafne* by Heinrich Schütz, employing the libretto of the first opera of all, Jacopo Peri's *La Dafne*, entertains Princess Sophie of Saxony and her wedding guests.

1742 Handel's *Messiah* redeems Dublin. 'The best Judges allowed it to be the most finished piece of Musick. Words are wanting to express the exquisite Delight it afforded to the admiring crouded Audience' (*Dublin Journal*).

1816 William Sterndale Bennett is born at Sheffield.

'There was a composer
    called Bennett
Whose career – it won't
    take long to pen it:
In his youth like a lark,
Up to Mendelssohn's
    mark,
He rose; since when,
    silent is Bennett.'
    (*Punch*).

1958 Van Cliburn, 23, of Texas, wins the first Tchaikovsky piano competition in Moscow.

Messianic music

1759 At 8 a.m. in London, Handel dies. 'He was sensible to the last moment; made a codicil to his will on Tuesday, ordered to be buried privately in Westminster Abbey, and a monument not to exceed £600 for him. I had the pleasure to reconcile him to his old friends; he saw them and forgave them, and let all their legacies stand! He died as he lived – a good Christian, with a true sense of his duty to God and man, and in perfect charity with all the world' (James Smyth to Bernard Granville).

1843 Two days after his 42nd birthday, Josef Lanner, co-founder of the Viennese waltz, succumbs to typhus.

1902 Maurice Maeterlinck, incensed at Debussy's choice of Mary Garden as Mélisande in preference to his own mistress, Georgette Leblanc, publicly disowns their opera in Figaro: 'The *Pelléas* under discussion is a piece which has become almost an enemy alien to me. Barred from all control over my work, I am compelled to wish that it fails resoundingly and instantly.'

1933 Electronic Morton Subotnick – 'I would sing mmmmmmmmmmSHA! into a tape recorder so that the sound could eventually come out zzzzzzLA' – is born in LA.

1915 Manuel De Falla's *El Amor Brujo* (*Love, the Magician*) is danced in Madrid.

1948 *Musique Concrète*, the musical application of recorded everyday sounds such as traffic noise and birdsong, is originated in Paris by a radio engineer, Pierre Schaeffer.

1959 Messiaen's *Catalogue d'oiseaux*, 13 piano pieces each describing a French bird in its natural habitat, is played in Paris by his wife, Yvonne Loriod.

1971 Stravinsky is laid to rest in Venice, beside his mentor Diaghilev.

1789 Mozart, from Dresden, anxiously to his wife: 'I beg you in your conduct to be careful of *your honour and mine,* but also to consider *appearances.* Do not be angry with me for asking this.'

1836 Verdi, 22, marries his sweetheart Margherita, daughter of the Busseto merchant who paid for his tuition.

1846 Domenico Dragonetti, 83, famed double-bass player, dies in London. 'His dog, Carlo, always accompanied him in the orchestra.' (G).

1851 Gounod's first opera *Sappho* moves Berlioz to tears. 'I threw my arm around him and said: "Oh, dear Berlioz, come and show those wet eyes of yours to my mother. No newspaper paragraph about my opera will make her half so proud."' (Gounod, *Autobiography*).

1973 Istvan Kertesz, 44, principal conductor of the London Symphony Orchestra, drowns while swimming off the Israeli coast.

 **14 APRIL**

 15 APRIL

 16 APRIL

17 APRIL

 18 APRIL

 19 APRIL

1764 Boasting that he has written as many books on music as he has years, historian and composer Johann Mattheson expires at 83.

1908 Emanuel Moór, inventor of a double keyboard and husband of a brewery heiress, plays his concerto in Boston. 'Whether it would not have been as profitable for him to tipple his ale in the shade is a question for posterity to decide,' comments Philip Hale in the *Boston Herald*.

1953 A Jerusalem fanatic attacks Jascha Heifetz with an iron bar, injuring his arm, for having played a Richard Strauss sonata banned in Israel because of the composer's brief association with Nazi institutions.

1689 Henry Purcell is ordered to surrender to the Dean of Westminster money that he enterprisingly earned from selling seats in his Abbey organ loft during the coronation of King William and Queen Mary.

1882 Leopold Stokowski, conductor, is born at Marylebone, London – a fact he conceals by faking his biography and accent.

1936 Ottorino Respighi, 56, falls to cancer in Rome, whose pines he orchestrally celebrated.

1944 *Fancy Free*, Leonard Bernstein's ballet of three sailors on leave in a Manhattan bar, goes down so well at the Met that he turns it into a musical, *On The Town*.

1768 Succeeding his godfather, Telemann, as cantor in Hamburg, C. P. E. Bach is daunted by the need to supply music for some 200 events a year.

1912 The *Jewish Chronicle* reports 'a notable triumph' – the first performance of *Rigoletto* in Yiddish. 'Little did Verdi imagine, when his work was first produced in Venice in 1861, that 61 years later it would delight the denizens of the East End in their own tongue. But such is the march of time ... Rigoletto cannot sound as well in Yiddish as in Italian. *"Caro nome del mio cor"* becomes *"Oisgekritzt in main hartz."'*

1950 Lord Berners, 66, composer, writer, and diplomat, dies at Faringdon Folly, the 140-foot tower he built near Oxford where guests sleep in crystal beds and are served food of uniform colour (the pigeons in the grounds are often dyed to match). His self-epitaph:
'Here lies Lord Berners
One of the learners
His great love of learning
May earn him a burning
But praise to the Lord
He seldom was bored.'

1862 Nikolay Rimsky-Korsakov, 18, graduates as a midshipman in the Tsar's Navy and embarks on a two-year voyage. 'Balakirev was deeply distressed by my impending departure and wanted to do some wire-pulling so as to have my sailing orders cancelled. But that was unthinkable.'

1869 A victim of apoplexy, lieder-composer Carl Loewe, 72, expires in Kiel.

1986 At 4.15 on a Sunday afternoon, the only hour he can respond to the muse, Vladimir Horowitz, 82, gives an internationally-televised recital at the Moscow Conservatoire, his first Russian appearance since emigrating 61 years previously. 'Do you have a message for the Russian people?' he is asked. 'Yes,' he replies, 'with my piano.' His personal Steinway grand has been flown in specially from New York.

1452 Cambrai Cathedral is so pleased with the music of Guillaume Dufay that it pays him a year's salary in advance.

1795 In the interval of a concert at Buckingham Palace, Joseph Haydn is presented to George III.

The King: Dr Haydn, you have written a great deal.

Haydn: Yes, Sire, a great deal more than is good.

The King: Oh no, the world contradicts that.

1831 Paganini, in an open letter, seeks vainly to refute reports that he is a convicted murderer in league with the Devil. 'One individual ... affirmed that he saw nothing surprising in my performance, for he had distinctly seen, while I was playing my [Witches'] variations, the Devil at my elbow directing my arm and guiding my bow.'

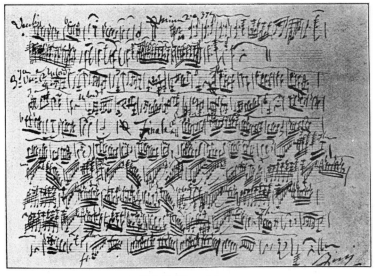

Diabolical Paganini score

21 APRIL

22 APRIL

 23 APRIL

 24 APRIL

1885 Dvořák conducts his Seventh symphony – 'a work which will shake the world' – in London.

1910 Schoenberg refuses to send greetings for Richard Strauss' birthday: 'He is no longer of the slightest artistic interest to me, and whatever I may once have learnt from him I am thankful to say I misunderstood.'

1916 Yehudi Menuhin, violinist, is born in New York City where his parents had migrated from Russia via Palestine. 'My mother took a vow: her child would wear a label proclaiming his race to the world. He would be called "the Jew"' (Menuhin, *Unfinished Journey*).

1984 A godson of Elgar's breaks 50 years' silence to identify the anonymous 13th *Enigma* variation as Helen Jessie Weaver, a Worcester lass to whom the composer was broken-heartedly affianced.

1891 Prokofiev believes he was born today in the Ukraine; his birth certificate says April 27.

1898 During Balakirev's First symphony, Rimsky-Korsakov shrugs his shoulders and flashes pitying smiles at his neighbours. The two composers never speak again.

1909 Balakirev's Second, based on a scherzo sketched 47 years earlier, is conducted by Liapunov.

1920 *The Excursions of Mr Broucek*, taking him in Janáček's opera up to the Moon and back to the 15th century, opens in Prague.

1792 In a fit of revolutionary ardour during the night, Claude-Joseph Rouget de L'Isle composes *La Marseillaise*, words and music, as a marching song for the French army of the Rhine.

1819 Rossini's *Eduardo e Cristina*, comprising seven new arias and bits from three earlier operas unknown to Venice, triumphs there. 'Rossini came in person to play the harpsichord. The people followed him about, cut off his hair "for memory"; then he was shouted, and sonnetted, and feasted and immortalised ...' (Byron).

1911 Alban Berg's Piano Sonata Op. 1 and String Quartet, Op. 3 – written in a fit of defiance when a publisher rejected the sonata – are played in Vienna.

1936 Bernard Van Dieren, 48, neglected Dutch composer, dies in London. 'As no mother bears children to see them blown to rags or choked in poison gas, so no composer plans his works for the monstrous fate of falling into the conventional concert programme ...' (Van Dieren, *Down Among the Dead Men*).

1865 Liszt takes minor holy orders and ever after wears an Abbé's cassock.

1904 Sibelius conducts his *Valse Triste* in Helsinki. It should have made his fortune, selling a quarter of a million copies in the piano version over the next 30 years, but he is tricked into accepting a royalty of barely 1 per cent.

1926 Puccini's *Turandot* is produced posthumously. As the composer's last note is heard, Arturo Toscanini lays down his baton, turns to the audience and announces: 'Here death stopped Puccini's hand.' The lights go up and La Scala empties silently.

1931 *Piér li houieu* (*Peter the miner*), a Walloon dialect opera by the great Belgian violinist Eugène Ysaÿe – who collapses at the first rehearsal and is too sick to conduct – opens in Brussels.

1827 The Royal Academy of Music, London, sacks its first general secretary and harp professor, the composer Nicholas Bochsa, on discovering that he is a forger, bigamist and bankrupt.

1891 Tchaikovsky docks in New York, checks into the Hotel Normandie and begins 'to walk up and down my rooms (I have two) and shed many tears.'

Ravel

1924 *The Times* dislikes *Tzigane*: 'The almost reptilian cold-bloodedness, which one suspects of having been consciously cultivated, of most of M. Ravel's music is almost repulsive when heard in bulk; even its beauties are like the markings on snakes and lizards.'

1749 Handel's Music for the Royal Fireworks is played at Green Park, London, in celebration of the peace treaty of Aix-la-Chapelle, but the squibs are so damp that a recriminatory sword-fight breaks out between the two organisers.

1810 Beethoven issues a popular piano piece 'For Elise, as a remembrance.' What he has really written is 'For Therese', but the publisher misreads his passionate dedication.

1867 Gounod's *Roméo et Juliette* opens at the Théâtre Lyrique with such impact that two months later it spawns a parody, *Rhum et eau en Juillet*.

1915 Alexander Scriabin, 43, dies in Moscow at 8.05 a.m. of a blood infection that spread from a fur-uncle on his upper lip.

25 APRIL

 26 APRIL

27 APRIL

28 APRIL

29 APRIL

30 APRIL

1865 Meyerbeer's *L'Africaine*, a romance of Vasco da Gama's global explorations, opens in Paris.

1865 Verdi rejects French criticism of an early opera: 'Some say I did not know Shachspeare when I wrote *Macbet*. Oh, in this they are greatly wrong. I may not have rendered *Macbet* well, but that I do not know, that I do not understand and do not feel Shachspeare, no, by God, no.'

1902 At the rowdy dress rehearsal of Debussy's *Pelléas et Mélisande*, the Minister of Education demands the excision of two lines alluding to a bed.

1940 Visiting Milan to hear her niece sing at La Scala, Luisa Tetrazzini, having squandered $5 million earned as a sensational soprano on a succession of worthless men, dies penniless aged 68.

1872 Cosima Wagner shuts the doors at Tribschen for the last time and sets out with her five children for Bayreuth, where Wagner awaits them.

1879 Thomas Beecham emerges at St Helen's, Lancashire, heir to a patent medicine industry for which he writes an Xmas jingle:
> 'Hark! the herald angels sing!
> Beecham's Pills are just the thing,
> Two for a woman and one for a child ...
> Peace on Earth and mercy mild!'

1899 Edward Kennedy ('Duke') Ellington, jazz symphonist, is born in Washington, D.C. and taught piano by a woman called Clinkscales.

1902 Agitators hoot Mary Garden's Scots brogue in *Pelléas et Mélisande* but Debussy is enthralled: 'Here was indeed the gentle voice I had heard in my inmost soul, with its faltering tenderness, the captivating charm I hardly dared hope for.'

1908 Serge Koussevitsky, using his bride's private fortune, founds a half-million-rouble publishing house, the Russian Music Edition.

1922 Plagued by syphilis (caught from her husband) and rumours of incestuous intimacy with her composer son, Rose Grainger plunges to her death from the 18th storey of a New York building. 'You and I never loved one another anything but purely and right,' she tells Percy in a final letter.

1940 Paul Hindemith, banned in Germany as 'degenerate' and a 'cultural Bolshevist', takes up a teaching post at Yale.

M * A * Y

1200 'The first of May,
  neither leaf nor
    beech
  nor song of bird
  nor gladiolus bloom
    pleases me,
  lady noble and gay,
  until I receive
  a speedy messenger
  from your fair self
  who will tell me
  the new delight
  which love brings
    me . . .' –
Troubadour Raimbaut de
Vaqueiras serenades his
Marquis's sister, Beatrice.

1786 'Mozart was as
touchy as gunpowder and
swore he would put the
score of his opera into the
fire if it was not produced
first.'[1] Happily, the
Emperor gives him prece-
dence over Salieri and
Righini, and *The Marriage
of Figaro* is staged in
Vienna.

1904 At lunch, Dvořák 'sat
down in his chair and ate
a plate of soup with
unusual zest. Scarcely
had he finished when he
said: "I feel kind of giddy.
I think I had better lie
down." These were the
Master's last words.'

[1]Michael Kelly.

1660 Alessandro Scarlatti
is born in Palermo.

1864 'I was greatly
annoyed by a man in the
next room who seemed to
be pacing up and down in
the most horribly squeaky
boots . . . I finally rang for
the porter and asked what
sort of caged lion it was' –
Singer Angelo Neumann,
in a Stuttgart hotel, hears
Richard Wagner prepare
to face his destiny.

1864 Working to the last
on his six-hour *L'Africaine*,
Giacomo Meyerbeer,
Wagner's arch-rival, dies
in Paris aged 72.

1936 Prokofiev's *Peter and
the Wolf* is given at a children's concert in Moscow.
A boy in the audience
writes: 'I liked best when
Petya fought with the
wolf and when all the
instruments played as
they caught the wolf.'

1956 Ralph Vaughan
Williams' Eighth
Symphony is aired in
Manchester by Sir John
Barbirolli.

1957 Tadeusz Kassern, 53,
composer and lately Pol-
ish cultural attaché in
New York, ends his life
after being denied US
resident status.

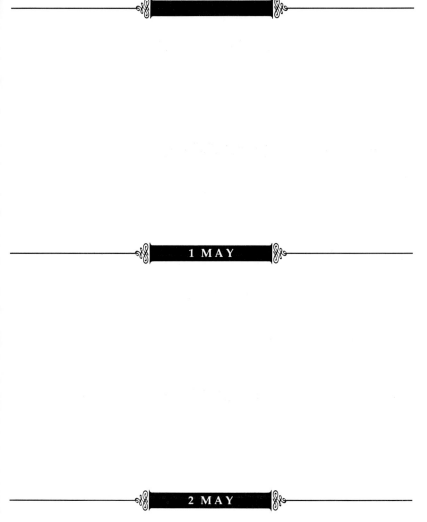

1 MAY

2 MAY

3 MAY

 **4 MAY**

 **5 MAY**

1864 At 10 a.m. in Stuttgart, the penniless, homeless Richard Wagner is presented with the signet ring of Ludwig II, new King of Bavaria. 'As this stone glows,' writes his saviour, 'so does the desire burn in him to meet the author and composer of *Lohengrin*.'

1911 Overcoming her father's objections to his 'Intellectual Inferiority, Impecuniousness, Shattered Health and The Moral Depravity of Members of my Family' (the last referring to his sister's unconcealed lesbianism), Alban Berg marries Helene Nahowski, statuesque daughter of a civil servant.

1952 A romance for harmonica and strings by Vaughan Williams is played in New York by Larry Adler. 'My first two performances of the work were, to understate things, lousy. That's because I am, and always have been, a bad reader; I learn better by ear.'

Ludwig II rides to the rescue

1860 Verdi, at the summit of his fame, begs his publisher, Ricordi, for a loan to renovate his house at Sant'Agata. 'For several years I have lived in the country in a hut, in such bad condition, so modest, so indecent, I would almost say, that I am ashamed to show it even to my most intimate friends.'

1874 A week after moving in at Bayreuth, Wagner names the house he built 'Wahnfried' ('Peace from Illusion').

1926 *Romeo and Juliet* is staged with deep cuts at Monte Carlo by Diaghilev, to the dismay of its 20-year-old English composer Constant Lambert. 'After the rehearsal the parts were collected, carefully corded and sealed and taken up in a strong room ... Now Diaghilev has spread the report that I went quite insane at Monte Carlo and had to be watched by 2 detectives' – Lambert to his mother.

1723 J. S. Bach signs a contract with the Leipzig Town Council, undertaking, as Cantor of St Thomas's School:
– To set the boys a good example of an honourable, disciplined way of life ...
– To show all due respect and obedience to the honourable Council ...
– To admit no boy to the school unless he already has a grounding in music ...
– To instruct the boys zealously not just in singing but in instrumental music, so that the churches may not be burdened with unnecessary expense.
– In keeping good order in the churches, to arrange the music that it does not last too long, and is of a style that does not produce an operatic effect but encourages the listeners to piety.'

1891 Tchaikovsky and Walter Damrosch conduct the opening concert at the hall Alexander Carnegie has built for the New York Oratorio Society.

1917 Debussy, dying of cancer, plays his violin and piano sonata with Gaston Poulet. 'His complexion was the colour of melted wax or of ashes. In his eyes there was no feverish flame but the dull reflection of silent pools.'

1814 At Darmstadt, Georg Joseph Vogler, 64, composer, cleric, organ builder and improviser extraordinary, is felled by a stroke.

'Well, it is earth with
  me; silence resumes
  her reign:
I will be patient and
  proud and soberly
  acquiesce.
... for my resting place
  is found,
The C major of this life:
  so, now, I will try to
  sleep.'[1]

1815 Paganini is arrested in Genoa for abducting and impregnating Angiolina Cavanna. He is released after ten days upon paying her father 1200 lire. The child is stillborn.

1897 Leoncavallo's *La Bohème* opens in Venice 15 months after being preempted by Puccini's.

[1]Robert Browning, 'Abt Vogler', 1864.

1747 Bach, 62, arrives in Berlin just as Frederick the Great is preparing for his nightly concert. 'With his flute in hand, he ... immediately turned to the assembled musicians and said, with a kind of agitation: "Gentlemen, old Bach is come." The flute was now laid aside ... The King gave up his concert for the evening and invited Bach to try his fortepianos, made by Silbermann, ... and to play unpremeditated compositions.'

1783 Mozart informs his father: 'Our poet here now is a certain Abbate da Ponte ... He has to write *per obbligo* an entirely new libretto for Salieri, which will take him two months, but has promised after that to write one for me.'

1824 Beethoven, conducting in a green coat, does not hear the triumphant reception of his Ninth symphony. Between movements, his contralto Caroline Unger 'plucked him by the sleeve and directed his attention to the clapping hands and waving hats and handkerchieves [sic].'

1825 Antonio Salieri, 74, passes away in an asylum: 'Mozart – I am said to have poisoned him; but no – malice, sheer malice; tell the world, dear Moscheles, old Salieri, who is on his deathbed, has told this to you.'

1833 Johannes Brahms enters the world at Hamburg. 'When I was a boy, I used to play in seamen's taverns all night long ... for drunken sailors and their girls.'

1840 Peter Ilyich Tchaikovsky is born to the second wife of the chief inspector of mines at Kamsko-Votkinsk, Vyatka province.

1926 *The Sorrows of Opera* by Milhaud is staged at Brussels.

1973 Benjamin Britten undergoes open heart surgery in London.

6 MAY

 7 MAY

8 MAY

9 MAY

10 MAY

1735 'And oh! ye active springs of life, Whose cheerful course the blood conveys, Compose awhile your wonted strife, Attend – 'tis matchless HANDEL plays ...'
On Mr Handel's performance on the Organ, *Grub Street Journal*.

1747 Having tested Frederick the Great's pianos, Bach is 'taken to *all* the organs in Potsdam'.

1924 Swiss composer Arthur Honegger advertises US railroads in his most successful work, *Pacific 2–3–1* (2 front trucks, 3 pairs of driving wheels, one rear truck). 'I have always loved locomotives passionately,' he declares in the printed score, 'as others love women or horses.'

1872 Giuseppina Verdi on her husband: 'He is a jewel among good men, he understands and experiences the most delicate and exalted sentiments, and yet this *rascal* dares to be, not an outright atheist, but certainly a man of little faith. And this with a calm obstinacy that is enough to make you want to pummel him.'

1884 Bruckner to a supporter: 'Please do not scold [the critic Eduard] Hanslick about me for *his rage is terrible*, it takes him to the verge of murder. One cannot fight him,

only approach him as a supplicant. *And I cannot even do that,* for he always refuses to see me ...'

1961 The first composition for synthesizer is presented by Milton Babbitt at Columbia University, New York.

Bruckner and the critics

1809 As Napoleonic troops advance to within cannon range of Haydn's home, the ailing composer tells his terrified servants: 'Don't be afraid, children; where Haydn is, no harm can reach you!'

1849 The Astor Place Opera House, New York, is wrecked by riots against the English actor William Macready, following London disturbances against Edwin Forrest, an American stage personality. In the fighting, 22 people die and 36 are wounded.

1894 On the night he conducts his first opera, *Guntram*, Richard Strauss announces his engagement to its principal soprano, Pauline de Ahna. Their 54-year marriage turns out to be 'so elemental in strength that none of Pauline's shrewish truculence could ever trouble it seriously.'

1941 German bombers destroy Queen's Hall, London's premier concert venue.

1809 Beethoven spends the night in his brother Caspar's cellar 'covering his head with pillows so as not to hear the [French] cannon,' afraid as much for his impaired hearing as for his life. Next day at 2.30 p.m. Vienna surrenders.

1865 Some 600 'friends from far and near' watch the dress rehearsal of Wagner's *Tristan and Isolde* but miss the premiere, delayed for a month by the hoarseness of its heroine, Malvina Schnorr.

1916 Composer Max Reger, 43, is found dead, holding a newspaper, in a Leipzig hotel room.

1832 With a plot used the previous year by Auber in *Le Philtre*, Donizetti conquers Milan with *L'elisir d'amore*.

1842 Jules Massenet is born at Montaud, France.
'To the music of
    Rimsky-Korsakoff
I could never take my
    corset off
And where are the
    sailors who would
    pay
To see me strip to Massenet?'
(Gypsy Rose Lee).

1845 At Pamier, southern France, Gabriel-Urbain Fauré shares his birthday. 'I grew up a rather quiet, well-behaved child in an area of great beauty ... but the only thing I remember really clearly is the harmonium in [the] little chapel. Whenever I could get away, I ran there and regaled myself ... I played atrociously.'

1884 Bedrich Smetana, 60, dies syphilitically insane.

1926 A first symphony in F minor, a graduation exercise by Dmitri Shostakovich, 19, is performed by the Leningrad Philharmonic.

1842 Inauspiciously on Friday the 13th and unfashionably at Lambeth, south London, Arthur Sullivan is born, son of a sergeant bandmaster.

1871 'We were then in open insurrection ... and M. Auber, still faithful to his beloved boulevard near the Passage de l'Opéra – his favourite walk – met a friend also in despair over the terrible days we were passing through and said to him,

in an accent of utter weariness,-
"Ah! I have lived too long!" Then he added with a slight smile, "One should never abuse anything."' In Communard Paris in his 90th year, comic-opera composer Daniel Auber surrenders his sprightly spirit.

1986 A sheet of Schütz, a Bach cantata, Haydn's 97th Symphony, Schubert's *An die Musik*, Freud's analysis of Mozart's coprophilia, all in the authors' autograph, are among 180 items presented to the British Library by the estate of Stefan Zweig, Austrian author, collector and librettist – the short score of his Strauss opera, *Die Schweigsame Frau*, is included in the bequest.

11 MAY

 12 MAY

13 MAY

14 MAY

 15 MAY

1847 Fanny Mendelssohn, pianist and composer, suffers a fatal stroke at the age of 41. Her younger brother, Felix, on hearing the news, 'with a shriek fell to the ground and remained insensible for some time.' Six months later he follows her to the grave.

1914 At the Paris Opéra, Richard Strauss conducts his *Josephslegende* but is not paid the agreed 6000 gold francs by Diaghilev.

1931 Arturo Toscanini is beaten up in Bologna for refusing to conduct the Fascist *Giovinezza* anthem. Crowds besiege his hotel shouting '*A morte* Toscanini!' and he flees under cover of night. His protest to Mussolini results in house arrest and the confiscation of his passport.

1960 'Announce to the audience when the piece will begin and end if there is a limit on duration. It may be of any duration. Then announce that everyone may do whatever he wishes for the duration of the composition.' Text of Composition 1960 3 by La Monte Young.

1501 Ottaviano Petrucci of Venice prints a book of music from movable type, founding the first music publishing imprint.

1567 Claudio (Giovanni Antonio) Monteverdi is born in Cremona, the son of a barber-surgeon. When barely 15, his motets are published in Venice.

Monteverdi

1858 With a dissertation *On the Analogy of Arsenic with Phosphoric Acid*, Borodin is awarded his doctorate in chemistry.

1920 *Pulcinella* in Paris marks the beginning of Stravinsky's neo-classical phase.

1792 The Teatro La Fenice opens in Venice with a Paisiello opera.

1849 A warrant is issued in Dresden for the arrest of the opera Kapellmeister, implicated in revolutionary activities. 'Wagner is 37 to 38 years old, of medium height, has brown hair, wears glasses; open forehead; brown eyebrows; eyes grey-blue; nose and mouth well-proportioned; chin round. Particulars: in moving and speaking he is hasty.'

1980 Under the slogan 'Keep Music Live!' British musicians vote to boycott the BBC until it abandons a plan to disband five regional orchestras. During the two-month strike, only recordings are broadcast.

1806 Étienne-Nicolas Méhul stages an opera, *Uthal*, without violins. 'Oh, to hear a cricket chirp,' sighs Grétry in the audience.

1866 Erik Satie is born at Honfleur, son of a French ship's broker and Scottish mother. 'An artist must regulate his life ... I rise at 7.18. I am inspired from 10.23 to 11.47. I lunch at 12.11 and leave the table at 12.14. A ride on my horse for my health's sake from 1.19 p.m. to 2.53.

Another bout of inspiration from 3.12 to 4.07 ... Symphonic readings (aloud) from 8.09 to 9.59. My bedtime regularly is 10.37. Every week I awaken with a start at 3.19 a.m. (Tuesdays) ... I only close one eye when sleeping.'

1890 Pietro Mascagni's *Cavalleria Rusticana (Rustic code of honour)*, wins a competition for one-act operas in Rome. 'Mascagni, appeared looking

very shabby in an old grey suit with trousers turned up ... His hair was long and unkempt, his face haggard and thin – evidently he had been starved and unwashed for weeks ... The poor young fellow (he is only 20 years old) probably that very morning was wondering how he could provide food for his wife and baby' (Lillie de Hegermann-Lindencrone).

1978 Philips announce the advent of Compact Disc.

1909 Isaac Albeniz, 48, who distilled the music of Spain in four volumes of piano music called *Iberia*, expires on the French side of the Pyrenees days after receiving the Légion d'Honneur from the hands of his friend, Granados.

1911 At 11.05 p.m. in the Loew sanatorium, Vienna, in the midst of a violent thunderstorm, Gustav Mahler breathes his last. He is 50 years old and alone, his wife having been sent out of the room. 'I can never forget his dying hours and the greatness of his face as death drew nearer. His battle for eternal values, his elevation above trivial things and his unflinching devotion to truth are an example of the saintly life' (Alma Mahler).

1917 Erik Satie's ballet *Parade* with a score that simulates the noise of typewriters and sirens, scenario by Jean Cocteau, opens in Paris to derisive reviews, Satie responds provocatively, is sued for defamation by a critic, Jean Poueigh, and sentenced to eight days' imprisonment. Cocteau slaps Poueigh's lawyer, is arrested and beaten in the cells. Writing in the programme, Guillaume Apollinaire coins the term 'surrealism'.

1764 Mozart, aged 8, plays for King George III and Queen Charlotte of England from 6 to 10 p.m. The Queen's music master, Johann Christian Bach, takes the boy upon his knee and plays a sonata with him, 'each in turn playing a bar with such precision that no one would have suspected two performers'.

1786 John Stanley, blind composer of famous organ voluntaries and seventh Master of the King's Musick, dies in London aged 73.

1861 Helen Porter Mitchell opens her lungs in Melbourne. Using diminutives of her Christian name and her birthplace, she becomes Nellie Melba.

1886 In London, Saint-Saëns directs his third and most successful symphony, with organ accompaniment, earning the soubriquet, 'the French Beethoven.'

1954 Charles Ives, 79, dies in New York.

17 MAY

18 MAY

19 MAY

20 MAY

 21 MAY

 22 MAY

1887 Chabrier's *Le Roi malgré lui* is killed off when the Opéra-Comique burns down two days after the premiere.

1896 The death of Clara Schumann, 76, stuns her faithful friend Brahms who races across Germany to miss by hours her funeral at Frankfurt, and barely glimpses the coffin as it is lowered into a grave beside her husband's at Bonn.

Clara Schumann

1950 Luigi Dallapicola is censured by the Roman Catholic church for his 12-tone opera *Il prigioniero* (*The Prisoner*), depicting the mental cruelties of the Inquisition.

1170 St Godric, illiterate composer of hymns dictated to acolytes, dies at Finchale, England, aged over 100.

1792 Felice de Giardini fiddles in London; 'like a pig,' notes Haydn.

1892 Leoncavallo's *I Pagliacci* opens at La Scala, Toscanini conducting.

1982 Beethoven's violin concerto appears on record with a dissonant cadenza by Soviet composer Alfred Schnittke containing snatches of many other concertos. The conductor, Neville Marriner, calls it, 'a contemporary fantasy of what Beethoven's thoughts might have been at the end of the 20th century.'

1986 Harrison Birtwistle's *Mask of Orpheus* is staged at English National Opera.

1813 Wilhelm Richard Wagner is born in Leipzig. 'My father was a police registrar who died six months after my birth. My step-father Ludwig Geyer was an actor and painter; he also wrote a few comedies ... The day before he died (I was 7) I had to play [piano] pieces to him from the next room; then I heard him say to my mother in a weak voice: "Do you think he has musical talent?" Next morning, after he had died, Mother came

into the nursery and said ... "He wanted to make something of you."'

1813 On the selfsame day in Venice, Rossini directs *The Italian Girl in Algiers*, his second success of the season.

1874 On the first anniversary of the death of Alessandro Manzoni, poet and patriot, Verdi offers his *Requiem* in the church of San Marco, Milan.

1950 *Four Last Songs* by Richard Strauss are sung in London by Kirsten Flagstad, eight months after the composer's death.

1789 Mozart, in Berlin, to his Constanze: 'On June 1st I intend to sleep in Prague, and on the 4th – the 4th – with my darling little wife. Arrange your sweet nest very daintily, for my little fellow deserves it indeed, he has really behaved himself very well and is only longing to possess your sweetest ... [blot]'

1881 Adorned with daffodils, Oscar Wilde flamboyantly attends the opening of Gilbert and Sullivan's aesthete-mocking *Patience*.
'Though the Philistines may jostle,
You may rank as an apostle
In the high aesthetic band
If you walk down Piccadilly
With a poppy or a lily
In your mediaeval hand.'

1912 Jean Françaix is born at Le Mans; he precociously publishes a piano suite when ten years old.

1803 Beethoven plays his new sonata with George Augustus Polgreen Bridgetower, a violinist of African and Polish extraction. On falling out with him, he dedicates it instead to Kreutzer, a French fiddler who finds it 'outrageously unintelligible' and never plays the piece.

1911 Elgar's Second Symphony is coolly received. 'What's the matter with them, Billy?' he complains to the orchestra's leader, 'they sit there like a lot of stuffed pigs.'

1918 Bartók's *Duke Bluebeard's Castle*, depicting the wife-murderer as a lonely and misunderstood idealist, is staged in Budapest.

1941 Songwriter Robert Allen Zimmerman is born at Duluth, Minnesota. As a university student in 1959, he adopts the surname Dylan.

1498 Ottaviano Petrucci of Venice, inventor of the earliest method of printing music, applies for exclusive rights to publish 'Figured Music and ... Plainchant: a thing very important to the Christian religion, and a great embellishment, and exceedingly necessary'.

1869 The opening of the Opera building in Vienna is clouded by the suicide of one architect and cardiac collapse of the other, after mild criticism of the Gothic edifice by Emperor Franz Joseph.

1965 'Xenakis' music makes Stockhausen sound like an old master' (New York *Herald Tribune* on the first all-Xenakis festival in Paris).

1984 *Samstag*, the second opera in Stockhausen's *Licht* cycle, is staged in Milan.

23 MAY

24 MAY

25 MAY

26 MAY

27 MAY

28 MAY

1861 After dinner in Paris at Halévy's, Liszt plays a 'horribly difficult' new piece that, he boasts, 'only two pianists in Europe can play as written and at the prescribed speed, Hans von Bülow and myself'. Whereupon young Georges Bizet moves into his seat and dashes off the toughest passage accurately from memory.

Verdi rides again

1870 'I have read the Egyptian scenario. It is well made,' writes Verdi, hooked by *Aïda*.

1924 Mounting the stairs to his doctor's surgery at 57 East 77th Street, Manhattan, Irish-American composer Victor Herbert (*Naughty Marietta*), suffers a fatal heart attack after a heavy lunch. He is 65 and weighs, according to the *New York Times*, over 250 pounds.

1730 Leonardo Vinci, composer (no relation), chokes in Naples after drinking a cup of chocolate supposedly poisoned by his loved one's brother.

1840 Paganini, 57, dies at 5.20 p.m. in Nice but is refused burial by the Bishop. He is finally laid to rest 36 years later at Parma.

1906 Mahler conducts his fatalistic Sixth at Essen. 'None of his works moved him so deeply at its first hearing as this. We came to the last rehearsals ... to the last movement with its three great blows of fate. When it was over, Mahler walked up and down in the artists' room, sobbing, wringing his hands, unable to control himself' (Alma Mahler).

1805 Luigi Boccherini, composer of 154 string quintets and 91 quartets, dies spitting blood in Madrid, aged 62. 'If God chose to speak to man he would employ the music of Haydn; but if He desired to hear an earthly musician he would select Boccherini.'

1904 Three months after its La Scala fiasco, Puccini takes ten curtain calls for the revised *Madama Butterfly* at Brescia.

1923 György Ligeti is born in Transylvania. 'When I was three years old I stayed with my aunt, a teacher, for three months ... When she realised I was afraid of spiders she made me collect cobwebs with bare hands. It terrified and disgusted me. Whether this explains ... the impenetrable web of sound, an original Ligeti invention, I cannot tell. My arachnophobia may have contributed to it.'

1934 Fritz Busch and *Figaro* open the first Glyndebourne Festival.

1910 At 6.30 a.m. of a severe cold, Balakirev, 73, dies in St Petersburg.

1911 Leaping in to his garden pond at Harrow Weald, Middlesex, to save Miss Ruby Preece from drowning, Sir William Schwenk Gilbert, 74, Sullivan's partner, suffers heart seizure and submerges. 'I should like to die,' he once mused, 'upon a summer day in my own garden.'

1913 Stravinsky's *Rite* turns into the Riot of Spring as affronted aesthetes arise in uproar. 'The theatre seemed to be shaken by an earthquake. It seemed to shudder. People shouted insults, howled and whistled, drowning the music, there was slapping and even punching. Words are inadequate to describe such a scene' (Valentine Gross). 'Exactly what I wanted,' says impresario Diaghilev afterwards.

1922 Iannis Xenakis is born of Greek parents in Rumania, by forceps delivery.

1942 For the soundtrack of a movie, *Holiday Inn*, Harry Lillis (Bing) Crosby records a song, 'White Christmas', that sells some 25 million copies, more than any other disc before or since.

1972 Margaret Ruthven Lang, Boston composer, dies at the age of 104.

1866 Smetana's *Bartered Bride* fails to impress at its Prague premiere. Over the next four years he revises it four times, creating the world's most popular Czech opera.

1958 Half a century after he gave it to the violinist Steffi Geyer – who kept the score but never played it – Bartók's first violin concerto is performed in Basle.

1962 Coventry Cathedral, razed in the Blitz, is consecrated anew with Benjamin Britten's *War Requiem*.

31 MAY

1809 Forty minutes past midnight, Joseph Haydn, 77, dies peacefully in the presence of his copyist, Johann Essler, and servants.

1905 Franz Strauss, principal horn in the Munich Court Orchestra and father of Richard, dies aged 83. Wagner found him 'an unbearable fellow ... but when he plays his horn, one cannot be cross with him.'

1959 Hailed as 'the first space opera', Karl Birger Blomdahl's *Aniara*, opening in Stockholm, is a sci-fi saga of nuclear winter escapees in an orbiting capsule.

1961 Krzystof Penderecki attracts universal attention with *Threnody for the Victims of Hiroshima*, broadcast by Warsaw Radio.

29 MAY

 30 MAY

 31 MAY

Pietro Mascagni

1 JUNE

2 JUNE

J * U * N * E

1804 Mikhail Ivanovich Glinka, the first Russian to win musical recognition – 'you and Weber are like two rivals courting the same woman,' says Liszt – is born at Novospasskoye, since renamed Glinka.

1809 Haydn's funeral. 'Not one Viennese Kapellmeister was in the cortège.'

1901 Universal Edition, foremost 20th century music publisher, is founded in Vienna.

1943 *Mous-Arechac* by a previously unknown Arab, Hamid al-Usurid, is played at the École Normale de Musique in occupied Paris. It is an anagram of *Scaramouche* by the exiled Jew, Darius Milhaud.

1969 The New York Philharmonic Orchestra appoints Pierre Boulez to succeed Leonard Bernstein as music director.

1857 In a cottage at Broadheath, a village near Worcester in the centre of England, Edward Elgar enters the world. His mother categorizes him:
> 'Nervous, sensitive & kind,
> Displays no vulgar frame of mind.'

1883 Three weeks short of her 30th birthday, Hedwig Reicher-Kindermann, magnificent Wagnerian soprano, is slain by a fever in Trieste.

Mascagni as Maestro

1911 *Isabeau*, Mascagni's reworking of the Lady Godiva legend, opens in Buenos Aires. 'We intended to have Isabeau appear naked,' he apologises, 'but not every soprano would consent. Besides, she might catch cold.'

117

1746 James Hook is born in Norwich with feet so cruelly deformed that only after several operations is he able to hobble. He becomes a famed organist.

1875 On his sixth wedding anniversary at 2 a.m., Georges Bizet dies heartbroken over *Carmen*'s failure. He is 36 years old.

1893 Dvořák heads for the summer to Iowa. 'In Spillville the Master scarcely ever talked about music and I think that was one of the reasons he was so happy there.'

1899 At 4.15 p.m. in Vienna, Johann Strauss II, 73, gives his last beat.

1947 *Les Mamelles de Tirésias* (*Tiresias' Tits*), Poulenc's transvestite opera after Apollinaire – who 'spent his first 15 years tied to his mother's frivolous petticoats' – is staged in Paris.

1787 Mozart buries his pet starling.

1904 *Flagellatenzug*, a symphonic poem by Karl Bleyle luridly depicting the self-mortification of medieval penitents, is beaten out in Munich.

1913 *Julien*, sequel to Gustave Charpentier's phenomenal *Louise*, opens amid great excitement in Paris and closes within a month.

1951 Serge Koussevitsky, tyrannical conductor, dies in Boston aged 76, 'There were times,' says one player, 'when I would gladly have forfeited my career for the pleasure of spitting in his face.'

1625 Waiting with King Charles I in Canterbury for his French bride to arrive, composer Orlando Gibbons, 42, suffers terminal apoplexy.

1826 Carl Maria von Weber, 39, is found dead in bed in London. 'An ulcer on the left side of the larynx, the lungs almost universally diseased, filled with tubercules of which many were in a state of suppuration, with two vomicae – one about the size of a com-

mon egg ... which was a quite sufficient cause of his death'. (Coroner's report).

1859 Verdi, on receiving bad notices: 'If an opera is bad, the journalists are right to speak ill of it; if it is good and they refuse to acknowledge the fact because of their own prejudice or other people's, one should let them talk and pay no attention.'

1961 Critic Hans Keller broadcasts twice in one evening on the BBC a hoax collage of random noises purporting to be a new work by an avantgarde Pole, Piotr Zak. 'The composer's refusal to publish a score suggests that he considers a consciously analytic approach a waste of the listener's time. It was certainly difficult to grasp more than the music's broad outlines' (*The Times*).

3 JUNE

 4 JUNE

 5 JUNE

6 JUNE

7 JUNE

1727 Fans of the rival sopranos Faustina and Cuzzoni jump on each other during a Bononcini opera at the Haymarket, 'and notwithstanding the Princess Caroline was present, no Regards were of Force to restrain the Rudeness of the Opponents.'

1869 '"A son has arrived!" ... He could clearly distinguish the lusty yells of the baby boy. With feelings of sublime emotion he stared in front of him, was then surprised by an incredibly beautiful, fiery glow which started to blaze with a richness of colour never before seen, first on the orange wallpaper beside the bedroom door ... The sun had just risen above the Rigi and was putting forth its first rays, proclaiming a glorious sun-drenched day. R. dissolved into tears.' Wagner, in Cosima's diary, greets the birth of his heir, Siegfried.

1935 Rudolf Wagner-Regeny's *Midsummer Night's Dream*, replacing the outlawed Mendelssohn's setting, is played in Nazi Düsseldorf.

1954 The skull of Joseph Haydn, taken from his coffin two days after the funeral, is reunited with his torso at Eisenstadt after going briefly on public display at the Friends of Music Society in Vienna.

Son Siegfried

1916 Ravel, serving as a military driver, publicly protests at the wartime ban on current Austro-German music, especially Schoenberg and Bartók: 'It is dangerous for French composers to ignore systematically the output of their foreign colleagues and to create a national coterie of arts.'

1933 *The Seven Deadly Sins of the Bourgeoisie*, written by Kurt Weill and Bertolt Brecht after fleeing Nazi Germany, causes uproar in Paris when a well-known local composer, Florent Schmitt, rushes to the platform shouting 'Vive Hitler!'

1934 Stravinsky undergoes an appendectomy.

1945 A month after the end of war, the premiere of Benjamin Britten's *Peter Grimes* signals the revival of British opera. 'He was a savage fisherman who murdered his apprentices and was haunted by their ghosts' – from E. M. Forster's account of Grimes that caught Britten's attention.

1739 Trouble among the eunuchs of Venice: at a holy convocation, Caffarelli strikes Reginelli with the bow of a double bass and is battered in turn with a piece of wood 'to the accompaniment of shrieks from the monks who were in the choir.'

1810 A Zwickau bookseller begets Robert Schumann.

1926 Dame Nellie Melba takes her final curtain at Covent Garden after singing Mimi in *La Bohème* at the age of 65.

1937 Carl Orff's *Carmina Burana*, a setting of medieval student songs, is sung at Frankfurt Opera.

1968 At his Aldeburgh Festival, Britten stalks out of Harrison Birtwistle's violent *Punch and Judy*. The two composers never meet.

1865 Carl Nielsen, Danish composer, is born on the island of Funen. 'The bees hum with a special Funen accent, and when the horse whinnies and the red cows low, why, anybody can hear that it is quite different from anywhere else ... The bells ring and the cocks crow in Funen dialect, and a joyous symphony issues from all the birds' nests every time the mother bird feeds her young' (Nielsen, *Song of Funen*).

1904 The London Symphony Orchestra is formed when forty musicians walk out of the Queen's Hall band after Henry Wood refuses to let them send deputies to rehearsal.

1909 'Hence loathed
 Melody!
 Divine Cacophony,
 assume
The rightful over-
 lordship in her
 room
And with Percus-
 sion's stimulating
 aid
Expel the Heavenly
 but no longer
 youthful Maid!'
From Charles Villiers Stanford's *Ode to Discord*, performed in London.

1865 In *Tristan and Isolde* at Munich, a young married couple, Ludwig and Malvina Schnorr von Carolsfeld, play the tragic lovers. King Ludwig is enthralled: 'What rapture! – *Perfect* ... To drown ... sink down – unconscious – highest bliss. Divine work!'

1899 Ernest Chausson, 44, French composer (*Poème d'amour et de la mer*) dies of injuries sustained when falling off his bicycle.

1921 Stravinsky's *Symphonies of Wind Instruments*, dedicated to the memory of Debussy, is heard in London. 'I had no idea Stravinsky disliked Debussy so much as this. If my own memories of a friend were as painful as Stravinsky's of Debussy seem to be, I would try to forget them ... His music used to be original; now it is aboriginal' (Ernest Newman, *Musical Times*).

8 JUNE

 9 JUNE

 10 JUNE

11 JUNE

12 JUNE

13 JUNE

1864 Richard Strauss is born in Munich. Hans von Bülow rechristens him Richard the Third: Wagner was the first, and none could be second to *him*.

1881 Smetana's *Libuse* opens the new National Theatre in Prague but he can no longer hear a note.

1892 On their silver wedding day at Bergen, Edvard and Nina Grieg are roused at dawn by a military band playing Bach's *Ein' feste Burg*, the signal for municipal merriment climaxing in fireworks and cannon salvos. He gives her a new piano piece, *Wedding Day at Troldhaugen*, Op. 65/6.

1960 'The musical events do not take a fixed course between a determined beginning and an inevitable ending' – Stockhausen's electronic *Kontakte* is spontaneously created at the concert hall of Cologne Radio.

1905 Gentle Gabriel Fauré, 60, is made head of the Paris Conservatoire in a compromise between reactionaries and Debussyists. 'Monsieur,' his predecessor warns, 'the Conservatoire, as its name implies, exists to conserve tradition.'

1917 Hans Pfitzner's *Palestrina*, operatic account of a greater composer's travails, is conducted in Munich by Bruno Walter, then sent 'on a propaganda tour to Switzerland to demonstrate to the world the high level of German operatic art in the third winter of the War'.

1947 Nina Makarova, wife of the composer Aram Khatchaturian, conducts her own symphony in Moscow.

1886 On Whit Sunday, five days after being declared insane and forcibly deposed, King Ludwig II of Bavaria, Wagner's benefactor, drowns mysteriously on a stormy night in Lake Starnberg. He is 41.

1911 *Petrushka* by Igor Stravinsky, 28, is staged by Diaghilev in Paris.

Late Stravinsky

1923 *Les Noces*, Stravinsky's portrait of a Russian village wedding, is danced by the Diaghilev troupe. 'Writing as an old-fashioned popular writer, not at all of the highbrow set . . . I do not know of any ballet so interesting, so amusing, so fresh or nearly so exciting' (H. G. Wells).

1986 Benny Goodman, 'king of swing', dies in Chicago aged 77.

1594 Orlande Lassus (Orlando di Lasso), 62, Franco-Flemish polyphonist, surrenders his soul in Munich, depressed by Jesuit killjoys.

'If all be true that I do think,
There are five good reasons we should drink:
Good wine, a friend or being dry,
Or lest you should be by and by,
Or any other reason why.'

1876 Délibes' *Sylvia* is danced in Paris. 'If I had known this music earlier,' says Tchaikovsky, 'I would not, of course, have written *Swan Lake*.'

1974 *Stockhausen Serves Imperialism* is the title of a new book by Cornelius Cardew.

1986 Douglas Young's *Ludwig*, 'fragments from a mystery', is danced at Munich.

1843 Birth of Edvard Grieg, great-grandson of a Scots fisherman. 'My music has a taste of codfish in it,' says Grieg, on his 60th birthday.

1891 Tchaikovsky asks his publisher to buy him a new instrument, the celeste, that he saw in Paris costing 1200 francs. 'I am afraid Rimsky-Korsakov and Glazunov might hear of it and make use of the new effect before I can.'

1928 Alexander Glazunov leaves to represent the USSR at the Schubert Centennial in Vienna, where he defects to the West.

1967 Musicians celebrate the Jerusalem wedding of pianist-conductor Daniel Barenboim, 24, and cellist Jacqueline Du Pré, 22.

1710 Handel, 25, becomes Kapellmeister at Hanover to the Elector, George Leopold, future King of England.

1863 'Old men, women and children are leaving the city . . . Our position in a few hours has become very critical. We cannot advance and I fear lest our retreat should be cut off. A militia regiment passes at quick-step; it is headed for the front . . . My tuner has lost his head; the two [pianos]

have disappeared and the express company declines to be responsible for them' – Pianist Louis Moreau Gottschalk turns up for a recital in Harrisburg, Pennsylvania, in the midst of the Civil War.

1961 Schoenberg's dream of *Jacob's Ladder* ascends posthumously in Vienna.

1973 *Death in Venice*, Britten's opera on the story Thomas Mann wrote while Mahler lay dying, is staged at Aldeburgh.

 **14 JUNE**

 15 JUNE

 16 JUNE

**17 JUNE**

18 JUNE

19 JUNE

1854 Henriette Sontag, Beethoven's sweet singer, dies of cholera in Mexico City at the age of 48.

1882 Igor Stravinsky enters the world at Oranienbaum, a seaside resort where his parents are tasting the early summer air.

1931 *Die Mutter*, the first quarter-tone opera, is performed on instruments designed by its Czech composer, Alois Hába. Although widely acclaimed, it is rarely performed because few singers can accurately hit the semi-demi tones.

1967 Korean composer Isang Yun and his wife are kidnapped in West Berlin, flown to Seoul and sentenced to life imprisonment for espionage. (They are released in 1969 under diplomatic pressure.)

1782 In Bath, composer William Herschel, 41, gives his last concert. Between (and sometimes during) performances he has discovered through his telescope the planet Uranus and can now earn his living as a professional astronomer.

1821 Weber's *Der Freischütz* is a hit in Berlin.

1840 Verdi's wife, Margherita, 25, follows their two children to the grave. 'I was alone! – alone! . . . Three loved ones had disappeared forever. I no longer had a family! And, in the midst of the terrible anguish, to avoid breaking a contract, I was compelled to write and finish a comic opera!'

1955 *Le Marteau sans Maitre*, Pierre Boulez's first masterpiece, is heard at Baden-Baden. 'It is my *Pierrot Lunaire*,' he says.

1717 Johann (74 symphonies) Stamitz, father of two composers and the four-movement format, is christened at Nemecky Brod, Bohemia. He, 'like another Shakespeare . . . without quitting nature, pushed art further than anyone had done before him' (Burney).

1820 Ludwig Spohr raises the first baton in England. 'Quite alarmed at such novel procedure some of the Directors would have protested against it; but when I besought them to grant me at least one trial, they became pacified. The triumph of the baton as a time-giver was decisive, and no one was seen again seated at the pianoforte during the performance of Symphonies and Overtures.'

1833 'At this moment Liszt is playing my *études*; I should like to steal from him the way he plays my own *études*' (Chopin).

1926 George Antheil's *Ballet Mécanique* for 8 pianos, a pianola, 4 xylophones, electric bells, propellers, 4 bass drums, tam-tams and siren, is performed in Paris. Says Ezra Pound: 'If America has given or is to give anything to general aesthetics, it is presumably an aesthetic of machinery.'

1819 Jacques Offenbach, comic composer, is born in Cologne; he calls himself 'O. de Cologne'.

1842 Summoned to Buckingham Palace to test the new organ, Mendelssohn finds Prince Albert and Queen Victoria playing his music.

Plucky Offenbach

1924 Picasso paints the curtain for Darius Milhaud's *Blue Train*, an *operette dansée* about the railway route of the idle rich from Paris to the Riviera.

1940 Jehan Alain, 29, conscripted French organ composer, is killed on patrol in Alsace.

1813 News of Wellington's victory at Vittoria reaches Vienna, where Beethoven is induced to compose a Battle Symphony containing British and French anthems for J. N. Maelzel's mechanical invention, the Panharmonicon.

1868 Wagner's *Mastersingers of Nuremberg* compete at Munich. Eduard Hanslick, the critic caricatured within, calls it 'not the creation of a real musical genius but of a clever speculator, an iridescent mix of half-poet and half-musician, who has devised a new system from a superficially brilliant but basically patchy talent. This system is erroneous in principle and, in its consequent application, unbeautiful and unmusical.'

1908 Nikolai Rimsky-Korsakov, 64, collapses at his summer home outside St Petersburg. His pupil Stravinsky composes a *Chant Funèbre*, remembering 'my Rimsky [as] deeply sympathetic, deeply and unshowingly generous, and unkind only to admirers of Tchaikovsky'.

1832 Verdi, 18, applies to study music at the Milan Conservatory; he is turned down because (a) there is no room, (b) he is the wrong age, and (c) Maestro Piantanida, professor of counterpoint, 'is of the opinion that he will prove mediocre'.

1910 Peter Pears, tenor and Britten companion, is born at Farnham.
   'There's no need for
     Pears
   To give himself airs;
   He has them written
   By Benjamin Britten.'
   (*Punch*).

1919 Julian Scriabin, 11-year-old heir of the composer and himself a budding preludist, drowns in the Dnieper River near Kiev.

1924 *Portsmouth Point*, William Walton's waterfront sketch, is played in Zurich.

20 JUNE

21 JUNE

22 JUNE

 **23 JUNE**

 24 JUNE

 25 JUNE

1860 Mussorgsky completes *St John's Night on a Bare Mountain*; Rimsky-Korsakov, editing it, desanctifies his title.

1939 The War Department in Washington compassionately cuts the marching cadence of the US Army from 128 steps per minute to 120.

1943 James Levine, music director at the Met, is born in Cincinnati.

1964 Herbert von Karajan, quitting after eight years as director of the Vienna State Opera, declares he will never work again in his native Austria.

1986 Ex-Met soprano Patricia Welting, 47, and her two daughters are found shot in Fresno, California; unemployed husband John Hollahan is dead of carbon monoxide poisoning in the garage; no other suspect is sought.

1901 Happy birthday, Harry Partch, inventor of the 43-note scale.

1935 Terry Riley, founder of minimalism, is born at Colfax, California. Terry Riley, founder of minimalism, is born at Colfax, California. Terry Riley, founder of minimalism, is born at Colfax, California. Terry Riley, founder of minimalism, is born at Colfax, California. Terry Riley, founder of minima

1943 Ralph Vaughan Williams conducts his Fifth Symphony, dedicated to Sibelius.

1767 Georg Philipp Telemann leaves more than 1000 unclassified cantatas, 120 concertos and 40 operas at his death in Hamburg aged 86.

1858 Bizet reports from Rome: 'There are no chaste women here above the price of one franc and most of the men will do anything that is asked of them for a few sous. The same applies to the upper classes, except that it is more expensive. There is not one woman here in a hundred who does not have a Cardinal, a Bishop or a Priest according to her standing.'

1910 A week after his 28th birthday Stravinsky's first ballet, *The Firebird*, is danced in Paris by the Diaghilev company.

1963 *A Frenchman in New York*, Darius Milhaud's belated riposte to Gershwin, is performed by the Boston Pops.

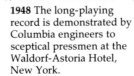

1933 Claudio Abbado is born in Milan, where he is first conductor at La Scala for 18 years; his father, Michelangelo, is a violinist and teacher at the Verdi Conservatory; his brother, Marcello, becomes its director.

1948 The long-playing record is demonstrated by Columbia engineers to sceptical pressmen at the Waldorf-Astoria Hotel, New York.

1982 André Tchaikovsky (no relation), 46, Polish-born pianist, endows the Royal Shakespeare Company with his skull, for use in the gravediggers' scene in *Hamlet*.

1729 Elisabeth-Claude Jacquet de la Guerre, composer, passes away in Paris. 'One can say that never had a person of her sex had such talents as she for the composition of music . . . She had an only son, who at eight years of age surprised those who heard him at the harpsichord . . . but death carried him off in his tenth year' (Titon du Tillet).

1941 The BBC adopts the four-note opening of Beethoven's Fifth symphony as a Morse signal of hope to Nazi-occupied Europe, conveying in code (. . . –) the letter 'V' for Victory.

1948 Some 56 years after he declared America uncultured and moved to Switzerland to paint pictures, ex-composer George Templeton Strong Jr expires at the age of 92.

1949 A symphony on the Robin Hood legend by Stalinist composer Alan Bush is performed at Nottingham.

28 JUNE

1491 Henry VIII of England, defender of one faith then founder of another, composer of two Masses, a motet and more than 20 songs, takes his first breath at Greenwich, outside London.

1838 During the coronation of Queen Victoria, Johann Strauss senior and his band stand outside the Reform Club playing *God Save the Queen*.

1841 *Giselle*, the ballerina's showpiece, is danced at the Paris Opéra by Carlotta Grisi to Adolphe Adam's music and a libretto by Théophile Gautier, who is madly in love with her but marries her sister.

26 JUNE

27 JUNE

28 JUNE

29 JUNE

30 JUNE

1801 Beethoven, 30, confesses: 'I have been avoiding all social functions simply because I feel unable to tell people: I am deaf. If I belonged to any other profession, it would not be so bad.'

1894 'Beg to report safe delivery of a strong healthy last movement to my Second [symphony]. Father and child both doing as well as expected – the latter not yet out of danger. At the baptismal ceremony it was given the name "The light shines in darkness". Silent sympathy is requested. Floral tributes are declined with thanks' (Gustav Mahler).

1910 The curator of the Liszt Museum at Weimar, in a jealous rage, slays soprano Anna Sutter, then himself.

1929 Carl Nielsen, in London, is summoned to tea with the Queen Mother and the Dowager Empress of Russia. Clutching borrowed dark trousers that do not fasten, he is ordered to give one arm to each noble lady as they go in to tea; the decencies are preserved by a valiant intake of breath.

1941 Ignacy Jan Paderewski, 80, pianist, composer and Polish Premier, dies in American exile.

1826 In the space of ten days, Schubert writes his final string quartet.

1879 After a benefit performance of his *Requiem*, Verdi dines with Giulio Ricordi, who casually refers to Shakespeare and Boito. Next day Boito submits a draft libretto. Verdi tells him: 'Write the poem. It will always do for me, for you, for someone else . . .'

1913 Erik Satie produces the first of three *Desiccated Embryos* for piano.

1960 *Oliver!*, Lionel Bart's Dickensian musical, opens in London and runs for 2618 performances.

Verdi rehearsing

J ∗ U ∗ L ∗ Y

---

1 JULY

1784 Wilhelm Friedemann Bach, 73, Johann Sebastian's eldest and brightest son, dies destitute in Berlin leaving a widow, a daughter and a shameful mess among his father's manuscripts, some of which he sought to pass off as his own.

1925 Erik Satie, 59, miniaturist and satirist, dies in a Paris hospital of cirrhosis of the liver. An inventory at his Arcueil apartment reveals a dozen unworn, identical corduroy suits, 89 freshly laundered handkerchiefs, a cigar box containing 4000 tiny drawings, and a derelict piano, its pedals tied on with string.

1977 *Every Good Boy Deserves a Favour*, Tom Stoppard's satire on abuse of human rights in Soviet psychiatric hospitals, opens in London, André Previn conducting his own score. Its initials form music's best-known mnemonic.

---

2 JULY

1591 Vincenzo Galilei, 71, composer, lutenist and advocate of ancient Greek music, is buried in Florence. His son, Galileo, is the famous astronomer.

1900 *Suomi*, a symphonic poem proclaiming Finland's right to self-determination, is emotionally received in Helsingfors. In Germany it is performed as *Vaterland*, in France as *La Patrie*. To avoid confusion, Sibelius renames the piece *Finlandia*.

1911 *Tristan* claims another life: Felix Mottl, Wagner's aide and editor of his vocal scores, collapses while conducting the opera in Munich.

1947 Winifred Wagner, English-born widow of Wagner's son, Siegfried, and his successor at Bayreuth, is convicted of abetting the cause of Nazism. She is stripped of 60 per cent of her property, sentenced to 450 days' community service and banned for life from running the Festival. Her sons, Wolfgang and Wieland, take over. .

Satie self-seen

3 JULY

 **4 JULY**

 5 JULY

1778 Mozart reports from Paris that his mother is seriously ill. In fact, she is dead and he is trying to break the news gently to his father, adding, 'You may have already heard that the godless arch-rascal Voltaire has snuffed it like a dog, like a beast. That is his reward!'

1854 In the Moravian village of Hukvaldy (pop. 570), not unlike the setting of his first successful opera, *Jenůfa*, Leoš Janáček is born, tenth child of the village schoolmaster.

1904 Twenty years after their elopement and soon after her husband's death, 'free of the impediment of crime and with no canonical impediment now existing', Puccini marries his companion Elvira.

1934 Rachmaninov, 61, recovering from minor surgery beside Lake Lucerne, starts weaving a rhapsody on a theme from Paganini's caprice No. 2 in A minor, previously improvised upon by Schumann and Brahms. Working dawn to dusk, he completes the quasi-concerto in six weeks.

1623 'Since singing is so
    good a thing
  I wish all men
    would learne to
    sing.'
William Byrd, unreformed Roman Catholic composer at the courts of Elizabeth I and James I, dies at Stondon Massey, Essex, aged 80.

1826 On the 50th anniversary of American Independence, at Lawrenceville, Pennsylvania, the first cry is heard from Stephen Collins Foster, whose ballads 'Oh Susannah', 'My Old Kentucky Home' and 'The Old Folks at Home' enter the national heritage.

1900 On this All-American day in New Orleans, trumpeter and singer Louis Armstrong is born. He is dubbed 'Satchmo' for Satchelmouth.

1931 On the iconoclastic 'Fourth of July' movement of his *Holidays Symphony*, Charles Ives instructs his copyist: 'Please don't try to make things nice! All the wrong notes are *right*.'

1855 Offenbach's Théâtre des Bouffes-Parisiennes opens with four comedies he has composed within a month.

1877 'I am going to be married,' homosexual Tchaikovsky tells his brother Anatol. 'Do not worry about me. I have thought it over, and am taking this important step in life with a quiet mind. You will realise that I am quite calm when I tell you – with the prospect of marriage before me – that I have been able to write two-thirds of my opera [*Eugene Onegin*].'

1897 Paul Ben-Haim, Israel's foremost composer, is born in Munich under the less euphonious surname of Frankenburger.

1941 Arturo Toscanini puts 11-year-old Lorin Maazel on to his podium for an adult concert with the NBC Symphony Orchestra, muttering, 'You're on your own, son.'

1812 Ludwig van Beethoven composes but does not mail the first of three letters to his Immortal Beloved – supposedly Antonie Brentano, a married aristocrat. 'My angel, my all, my very self . . . Why this profound sorrow when necessity speaks – can our love endure without sacrifices, without our demanding all from one another; can you alter the fact that you are not wholly mine, as I am not wholly yours?'

1937 Vladimir Ashkenazy, pianist and conductor, is born in Gorky; he flees Russia at the age of 26. 'I know for sure that my mentality is no longer that of a Soviet; I believe in free will.'

1954 Entering a record studio for the first time, Elvis Aron Presley, 21, sings 'That's All Right, Mama' and 'Blue Moon over Kentucky'.

1973 Otto Klemperer, towering German conductor – 'I am the last of the classical school: when Bruno Walter died I put my fees up' – dies in Zurich aged 88.

1720 Bach's first wife, Maria Barbara, 36, is buried at Cöthen as he, unaware of her sudden death, plays for princes at Carlsbad. With six infants to raise, he remarries within 18 months.

1860 Gustav Mahler is born in the Bohemian village of Kalischt to ill-matched parents. 'They belonged together like fire and water. He was all stubbornness, she gentleness itself. Yet had it not been for their union, neither I nor my Third Symphony would exist: I find that thought remarkable.'

1911 Gian-Carlo Menotti starts life at Cadegliano, Italy, and writes two operas before he is 15.

1976 Tippett's fourth opera, *The Ice Break*, at Covent Garden confronts seemingly irreconcilable differences between East and West, black and white, old and young.

1746 Handel begins *Judas Maccabaeus*, in celebration of England's defeat of the Scots at Culloden.

1791 Oxford bestows a doctorate on Haydn. 'I had to pay 1½ guineas for having the bells rung at Oxforth in connection with my doctor's degree and ½ a guinea for the robe. The trip cost 6 guineas' (Haydn's diaries).

1880 Debussy, 17 and claiming to be 20, is engaged as a piano tutor for the summer by Nadezhda von Meck, Tchaikovsky's discreet benefactress.

6 JULY

 7 JULY

 8 JULY

9 JULY

**10 JULY**

11 JULY

1747 Giovanni Bononcini, 77, Handel's London rival, expires in Vienna.

> 'Some say, compar'd to Bononcini,
> That Mynheer Handel's but a ninny;
> Others aver that he to Handel
> Is scarcely fit to hold a candle:
> Strange all this difference should be
> 'Twixt Tweedle-dum and Tweedle-dee.'

1876 'Early yesterday morning Brahms came up to go bathing with me . . . I greatly admired Brahms' burly, well-knit and muscular body, though I fear it is too much inclined to stoutness . . . His solid frame, the healthy dark-brown colour of his face, the thick hair just a little sprinkled with grey, all make him appear the very image of strength and vigour' (Sir George Henschel's vacation diaries).

1906 Edwin Landseer Lutyens, architect of New Delhi and much else, fathers at 8.30 a.m. a fourth child, Elizabeth, who announces her destiny as a composer by driving burglars from 29, Bloomsbury Square with her first sounds.

1733 In Oxford, a day later than scheduled because 'the solemnity in conferring the Degrees . . . engag'd the Theatre to a very late hour', Handel presents his 'spick and span new oratorio *Athalia*'.

1798 Haydn starts his Nelson Mass in honour of the British Admiral who, while it is written, defeats Napoleon on the Nile.

Ailing Chopin

1848 'He accomplishes enormous difficulties, but so quietly, so smoothly and with such constant delicacy and refinement that the listener is not sensible of their real magnitude' (London *Daily News* on Chopin's final recital there).

1889 'Amen, so be it! We'll write this *Falstaff* then! For the moment we won't think of obstacles, of age, of illness!' – Verdi, 75, sets about his last opera.

1626 Nicholas Lanier becomes the first Master of the King's Musick, serving Charles I of England until his execution.

1862 Liszt receives a visit from Pope Pius IX, who calls him 'my dear Palestrina' and wonders whether his music could not be used to lead hardened criminals to repentance.

1937 George Gershwin, 38, dies in Hollywood under the surgeon's knife, of a brain tumour. 'I had to live for this,' he complains a few days earlier, 'that Sam Goldwyn should say to me: "Why don't you write hits like Irving Berlin?" '

1943 Benjamin Britten and Peter Pears give a recital for convicts at Wormwood Scrubs jail, west London. Turning their pages is Michael Tippett, serving a three-month term for breaking the terms of his exemption from military service as a conscientious objector.

1895 Kirsten Flagstad, towering Wagnerian soprano, is born at Hamar, Norway, but does not sing outside Scandinavia for another 38 years.

1900 Fauré's *Requiem* is given for the first time with full orchestra as part of the World Exhibition in Paris. 'It is as GENTLE as I am myself,' he reflects. 'Someone has called it a lullaby of death.'

1918 The Bolshevik government nationalizes the music conservatories of Moscow and Petrograd.

1946 Kathleen Ferrier makes her stage debut, creating the victim's role in Britten's *Rape of Lucretia* at Glyndebourne.

1976 *We Come to the River* by Hans Werner Henze, a manifesto for Marxist revolution, is staged at the Royal Opera House, London.

1881 Janáček, 27, marries. His bride is 15 years old.

1900 'What has opera to do with a lustful man chasing a defenceless woman?' – press comment on the British premiere of *Tosca*.

1935 Richard Strauss is sacked as head of the Nazi Reichsmusikkammer for uttering ideological heresies in an intercepted private letter to his librettist, Stefan Zweig. 'Do you believe Mozart composed as an "Aryan"? . . . Do you believe that I am ever, in any of my actions, guided by the thought that I am "German"?'

1943 Kurt Huber, 39, ethnomusicologist at Munich University, is beheaded by the Gestapo for disseminating anti-Hitler literature.

1951 Fifteen minutes before midnight on Friday 13th, a date he has long dreaded, Arnold Schoenberg, the man who liberated music from the constraints of tonality, dies at his Los Angeles home aged 76. Anna Mahler, sculptress daughter of his mentor, takes his death mask.

1789 'Oh God! I can hardly bring myself to dispatch this letter – yet I must! If this illness had not befallen me, I should not have been obliged to beg so shamelessly from my only friend. Yet I hope for your forgiveness, for you know both the good and bad prospects of my situation. The bad is temporary; the good will certainly persist . . .' Mozart to his lodge brother Baron Michael von Puchberg, who lends him the equivalent of £10,000.

1888 Jesse L. Lippincott, a Pittsburgh businessman, founds the first record company, the North American Phonograph Co.

1919 Diphtheria kills Chouchou, 14, Debussy's only child and inspiration of *Children's Corner*.

 **12 JULY**

 13 JULY

 14 JULY

15 JULY

 16 JULY

17 JULY

1876 'I read out from a Berlin paper the news of the death at Bayreuth of a member of the Wagner orchestra. "The first corpse," said Brahms drily' (George Henschel's diaries).

1929 Dressing for the funeral of his elder son, Franz, a suicide, Hugo von Hofmannsthal, 55, Richard Strauss's 'beloved poet', collapses and dies. On his desk, unopened, lies Strauss's telegram: 'First act [*Arabella*] excellent. Many thanks and congratulations.'

1930 Leopold Auer, 85, teacher of two generations of Russo-Jewish virtuosi – among them Heifetz, Elman, Zimbalist and Milstein – dies near Dresden.

'When we began
Our notes were sour –
Until a man
(Professor Auer)
Set out to show us, one and all,
How we could pack them in, in Carnegie Hall.'
(George Gershwin, *Mischa, Jascha, Toscha, Sascha*).

1934 Harrison Birtwistle is the first composer to be born in the Lancashire mill town of Accrington.

1782 Mozart's opera *Die Entführung aus dem Serail* (*The Abduction from the Seraglio*) succeeds in Vienna, despite hissing from an opposing faction. Afterwards, Emperor Joseph II observes, 'Too many notes, my dear Mozart.' To which the composer replies, 'Exactly as many as are needed, your Majesty.'

1927 Bartók, having a prodigious year, premieres his Piano Sonata at Baden Baden.

1948 Pinchas Zukerman, violinist, is born in Tel Aviv. 'Pinky was a brassy kid. He put his two feet down, stared you in the eye and dared you not to like it' (Isaac Stern, *New York Times*, 1 March 1979).

1717 To allay his unpopularity with the English, whose language he will not speak, Hanoverian George I throws a public concert on the River Thames for Handel to direct his *Water Music*; His Majesty likes the hourlong suite so much that he orders two full repeats.

1722 Hamburg councillors censure church Cantor Georg Philipp Telemann for having his music played 'in a public inn, whereby all manner of disorder is possible, and moreover making free to perform operas, comedies and all manner of entertainments likely to arouse bawdiness, even outside market days.'

1858 Urged by Balakirev to become a full-time composer, Modest Mussorgsky resigns his post in the Russian civil service.

1896 Bruno Walter visits Gustav Mahler at his summer retreat, Steinbach am Attersee. 'When, on our way to his house, my glance fell on the Höllengebirge whose forbidding rocky walls formed the background of an otherwise charming landscape, Mahler said: "No need to look there any more – that's all been used up and set to music by me." '

1723 Weeks after taking office as cantor at St Thomas's Church, Leipzig, Bach creates a magnificent motet, *Jesu, meine Freunde*, for the funeral of a chief postmaster's widow.

1872 Balakirev, dejected at the financial failure of his Russian concert society, goes to work as a clerk on the Warsaw railway.

1877 Tchaikovsky unlovingly weds Antonina Ivanovna Milyukova, 28, and takes her to St Petersburg. 'When the carriage started I was ready to cry out with choking sobs. Nevertheless I still had to occupy my wife with conversation as far as Klin in order that I might earn the right to lie down in my own armchair when it was dark and remain alone by myself.'

1927 The *Mahagonny Songspiel*, first fruit of the Brecht-Weill partnership, is staged at the highbrow Baden-Baden Festival. The demonstration began as we were singing the last song and waving placards – mine said "For Weill" – with the whole audience on its feet cheering and booing and whistling. Brecht had thoughtfully provided us with whistles of our own, so we stood there defiantly whistling back' (Lotte Lenya).

1842 'Buckingham Palace is the only friendly home in England' – Mendelssohn, to his mother.

1888 Hugo Wolf, 28, inserts the first of many coded messages in the personal columns of the *Neue Freie Presse* to contact his secret love, Melanie Köchert, wife of his benefactor.

Wooing Wolf

1903 'I met Debussy at the Café Riche the other night and was struck by the unique ugliness of the man. His face is flat, the top of his head is flat, his eyes are prominent – the expression veiled and sombre . . .' (James Gibbons Huneker, in the New York *Sun*).

1986 A modernist *Fidelio* is hissed as Sir Colin Davis, 58, ends a record 15 years as music director of the Royal Opera House, Covent Garden.

1812 Goethe reports taking a drive with Beethoven: 'His is a personality utterly lacking in self-control; he may not be entirely wrong in thinking the world odious, but that attitude does not make it any more pleasant for himself or for others.'

1909 'Yesterday I whipped myself as I have never before been whipped in my life . . . It lasted perhaps 10–15 minutes and when I had finished there were surely over 1000 long red stripes on me . . . The pains are quite unimportant after the first beginnings, only amusing, ecstatic, carried away, world-forgotten. Whipping is still lovely on all places but for me most ravishing on the breasts . . .' – Percy Grainger to his girlfriend Karen Holten.

1924 Schoenberg's Serenade Op. 24, the first work fully composed by the 12-tone method, is introduced at a chamber music festival in Donaueschingen.

18 JULY

 19 JULY

 20 JULY

21 JULY

22 JULY

23 JULY

1812 'In the evening, at Beethoven's. He played deliciously' – Goethe, in his diary.

1838 In his berth on the USS *Otis* bound for North America, Johann Nepomuk Maelzel, 65, inventor of the metronome, is found dead. He had wanted Beethoven to mark all his music by the metronome but was sharply told: 'It's silly stuff: one must feel the tempi.'

1865 Three weeks after singing *Tristan* for the fourth time, Ludwig Schnorr von Carolsfeld, 29, dies suddenly. 'Console Richard!' he cries at the last. 'For me he lived, for me he died,' comments Wagner.

1833 At the opening of Cherubini's last opera, *Ali Baba*, Berlioz towards the end of the first act shouts out: 'Twenty francs for an idea!' He doubles the offer in the middle of the second act and quadruples it in the finale, but finds no takers.

1847 *I Masnadieri* is premiered in London, with Verdi conducting and Jenny Lind as Amelia. 'The music,' notes Queen Victoria in her diary, 'is very inferior and commonplace.'

1870 Josef Strauss, 42, prince of more than 300 waltzes, expires in Vienna of a brain haemorrhage. 'He was the most gifted one of us,' says brother Johann, 'I am merely the popular one.'

1919 Manuel De Falla enters the limelight with a ballet of marital jealousy, *The Three-Cornered Hat*, danced in London by the Diaghilev company.

1757 Domenico Scarlatti, the first keyboard artist to cross hands while playing, dies in Madrid aged 71, having composed 555 sonatas.

1900 Alban Berg suffers a serious asthma attack, noting that 23 is his fateful number.

1912 Ethel Smyth, opera composer, is arrested in London for throwing a brick through the Home Secretary's window and setting fire to the Colonial Secretary's country home as tokens of her support for women's voting rights.

1979 'Music is no different from opium. Music affects the human mind in a way that makes people think of nothing but music and sensual matters. Opium produces one kind of sensitivity and lack of energy, music another kind . . . Music is a treason to our country, a treason to our youth, and we should cut out all this music and replace it with something instructive' – Ayatollah Khomeini, Ramadan exhortation to revolutionary masses in Teheran.

1739 Benedetto Marcello, described on his tombstone as 'the Michelangelo of music', dies at Brescia aged 53.

1880 Ernest Bloch, composer of American and Hebrew national epics, is born in Geneva, the son of a clockmaker.

1905 Claude Debussy moves into the Grand Hotel, Eastbourne, for two months to finish *La Mer* and begin *Images*. The sea, he finds, displays 'a strictly British correctness'.

1938 At the age of 74 Richard Strauss gives his first operatic premiere in his native Munich but the anti-war theme of *Friedenstag* (*Day of Peace*) dismays the Nazi authorities.

1825 Schubert, pleased by the reception of *Suleika*, warns his father not to be overjoyed: 'A review, however favourable, can be ridiculous if the critic lacks average intelligence, as is not infrequently the case.'

1900 Gustav Mahler makes a discovery. 'I see it more and more: one does not compose, one *is* composed!'

1976 *Einstein on the Beach*, Philip Glass's surrealist opera on the father of relativity, is staged at the Avignon Festival in France. The composer earns his living as a furniture remover, plumber and New York taxi driver.

1859 Jules Massenet, 17, wins the Grand Prix de Rome for his pianism.

1882 *Parsifal*, Wagner's 'sacred festival drama' and last opera, is staged at Bayreuth. Liszt finds it miraculous, but other loyalists complain of 'a lack of creative power'.

1888 Rimsky-Korsakov completes *Sheherazade*.

1908 Arnold Schoenberg writes the second movement of his second string quartet, abandoning tonality to weave variations around a folk tune ending 'all is lost': his wife, Mathilde, has eloped with his neighbour and painting teacher, Richard Gerstl.

 **24 JULY**

 25 JULY

 26 JULY

27 JULY

 28 JULY

 29 JULY

1819 Antonio Salieri, 69, on a stroll around Schönbrunn 'speaks with delight of a *Requiem* that he wrote under the notion that he would soon follow his wife, who died in 1807, but as this has not yet taken place, he has now written a much shorter one, thinking it was good enough for him'.

1871 Wagner, composing: 'Do you know what I have done today? Thrown out everything I did yesterday.'

1918 Gustav Kobbé, 61, author of the *Complete Opera Book*, is killed by a US Navy seaplane while sailing his boat off Long Island.

1924 At the line 'If only I could pray. Where are the words I knew once? They're dancing in my brain like . . .' in his opera *Doktor Faust*, Ferruccio Busoni, 58, dies in Berlin.

1741 Newly arrived from Venice, Antonio Vivaldi, 63, dies in Vienna at the house of a saddler's widow and is buried unceremoniously on the same day.

1750 Johann Sebastian Bach, 'just after a quarter to nine, in the 66th year of his life, by the will of his Redeemer, died quietly and peacefully'.

1896 'What joy and relief: Mahler's Third is finished!'

1941 Riccardo Muti, conductor, is born in Naples and soon moves to remote Molfetta. 'Until television came it was like living in ancient Greece : . . . We spent our time like Aristotle and Plato, teachers and students, discussing politics, history and philosophy' (Muti/NL).

1830 Berlioz, 26, quickly finishing a cantata, is 'free to maraud about the Paris streets, pistol in hand, with the "blessed riffraff", directing in the thick of revolution a mass singing of the *Marseillaise*'.

1856 Robert Schumann, 46, expires in an asylum near Bonn. 'I cannot again experience anything so touching as the reunion [after 2½ years] of Robert and Clara. At first he lay a long time, eyes closed, and she kneeled in front of him, more quietly than one would have thought possible. But he recognised her . . . once he wanted plainly to embrace her and threw his arms around her. Of course, he was no longer able to speak . . . He refused the wine that was offered him but took it eagerly from her finger, so prolongedly and hungrily that one was certain he recognised the finger' (Brahms, on Schumann's last days).

1970 Sir John Barbirolli, Anglo-Italian conductor of the New York Philharmonic Orchestra and Manchester's Hallé, dies in London aged 70.

1826 Beethoven's worthless nephew, Karl, pawns his watch and with the money buys two pistols, powder and balls which, next morning among the ruins of Rauhenstein outside Vienna, he discharges at his left temple but barely grazes the skin. It is his uncle who is shattered by the incident.

1829 Mendelssohn, sitting in the ruined, roofless Edinburgh chapel where Mary Stuart was crowned Queen of Scotland, conceives the opening bars of his *Scottish Symphony*.

1928 Janáček, 75, sets off for a fateful holiday in Hukvaldy with his love-object*, Kamila Stösslová, her husband and their 11-year-old son.

* I have recently pursued this matter exhaustively with scholars in Brno, and regret to report no evidence of consummation.

1750 M. Johann Sebastian Bach, Musical Director and Singing Master of the St Thomas School, was carried to his grave in the hearse.' 200 years later, his remains are moved inside St Thomas's Church.

1886 Liszt, 74, dies at Bayreuth. 'The Wagner family gave no outward sign of mourning. The daughters [his grandchildren] wore black dresses and that was all . . . Not even the receptions in Villa Wahnfried were interrupted. Everything was made to look – as if on purpose – that Franz Liszt's passing was not of sufficient importance to dim the glory of the Festival even temporarily by a veil of mourning' (Felix Weingartner: *Memoirs*).

1914 Told that his librettist has enlisted in the Austrian Army, Richard Strauss protests: 'Poets should be permitted to stay at home. There is plenty of cannon fodder available: critics, stage producers who have their own ideas, Molière actors &c. I am convinced there will be no world war, the little altercation with Serbia will soon be over and I will receive the third act of my *Frau ohne Schatten*. May the devil take the damned Serbs.'

Liszt unlamented

30 JULY

 31 JULY

August is the second of five names given to César
(Auguste Jean Guillaume Hubert) Franck.

1 AUGUST

2 AUGUST

A • U • G • U • S • T

1 AUGUST

1740 'Rule Britannia!' is first heard in Thomas Arne's masque, *Alfred*. It later crops up in works by Handel, Beethoven and Wagner.

1892 John Philip Sousa, 37, quits as leader of the US Marine Corps band and forms his own 100-man military band to play his famous marches.

1969 *Peking Review* reports the cleansing of Peking Opera. 'After the propaganda team entered this theatre, it followed Chairman Mao's instructions to "thoroughly criticise and repudiate reactionary bourgeois ideas".'

1973 Gian Francesco Malipiero, editor of the complete works of Monteverdi and many of Vivaldi's, dies at Treviso aged 91, outliving his own compositions.

2 AUGUST

1891 Mark Twain reports from Bayreuth: 'I wish I could see a Wagner opera done in pantomime once. Then one would have the lovely orchestration unvexed to listen to and bathe his spirit in, and the bewildering beautiful scenery to intoxicate his eyes with, and the dumb acting could not mar these pleasures, because there is not often anything in the Wagner opera that one would call by such a violent name as acting . . . This present opera was *Parsifal* . . . The first act of the three occupied two hours, and I enjoyed that in spite of the singing.'

1921 Enrico Caruso, inimitable tenor, dies in Naples aged 48. A great singer, he once said, is 'a big chest, a big mouth, 90% memory, 10% intelligence, lots of hard work and something in the heart'.

1945 Pietro Mascagni, wildly successful at 27 with *Cavalleria Rusticana*, fades away in a cheap Rome hotel aged 81, ostracized for playing a visible role in the Mussolini era.

1778 Salieri inaugurates La Scala with *Europe riconosciuta*.

1779 Mozart writes the Posthorn serenade.

1829 Rossini, 37, presents *William Tell* in Paris and announces it as his last opera.

1936 The 100-year ban on Schumann's Violin Concerto, in which Clara found 'definite traces' of madness, is rescinded in Berlin by the son of Joseph Joachim, for whom it was written.

1957 Cellist Pablo Casals, 80, marries his 20-year-old pupil, Martita Montanez, in Puerto Rico. 'The cello is like a beautiful woman who has not grown older but younger with time, more slender, more supple, more graceful' (Casals, interview in *Time* magazine).

1782 Mozart, 26, weds Constanze Weber, 19. 'When we were joined together, my wife began to weep and I too – and indeed they *all* wept, even the priests themselves at witnessing our emotion.'

1831 Berlioz finishes the first part of his Op. 18 *Tristia* 'in Rome on a day when the spleen was killing me'.

1930 After a *Götterdämmerung* rehearsal, Siegfried Wagner, 61, collapses and dies at Bayreuth.

1778 Thomas Linley junior, 22, promising composer, friend of Mozart and Sheridan's brother-in-law, drowns while boating in Lincolnshire.

1900 Mahler finishes his Fourth Symphony. 'As usual, he is not overjoyed: rather, profoundly depressed at losing the meaning it gave to his life.'

1916 George Butterworth, 31, composer and *The Times* music critic, is killed soon after capturing a German trench in the Battle of the Somme.

1920 Electronic music is heard when inventive cellist Leon Theremin presents his Thereminovox at the Moscow Technological Institute.

3 AUGUST

  4 AUGUST

  5 AUGUST

 6 AUGUST

 7 AUGUST

 8 AUGUST

1876 Past midnight, amid pathological privacy, Ludwig of Bavaria arrives at Bayreuth for the inaugural *Ring*. He departs secretively after viewing the dress rehearsals. 'I am coming to feast myself enthusiastically on your great work and to refresh myself in heart and spirit, not to be gawked at by the curious, or offer myself as an ovation-sacrifice.'

1914 Two days after war is declared, Australian Percy Grainger prays that 'the German soldiers will show themselves just as untalented as the German musicians'.

1962 'Last year, more Americans went to symphonies than went to baseball games. This may be viewed as an alarming statistic' – John F. Kennedy at a White House concert.

1750 Meeting to discuss the vacancy that has arisen, Leipzig town councillors agree that Herr Bach has been 'a great musician, but not a schoolmaster'.

1829 A day before visiting Fingal's Cave in the Inner Hebrides, Felix Mendelssohn writes the first 20 bars of his famous overture.

1893 Alfredo Catalani, whose opera *La Wally* so impresses his friend Toscanini that he names his daughter after it, succumbs aged 39 to tuberculosis.

1986 In *Yan Tan Tethera*, his second opera in four months, Harrison Birtwistle illustrates north–south antagonism in a contest between two numerological shepherds.

1857 Cécile Chaminade, lady composer of *Les Amazones*, is born in Paris.

1874 Mussorgsky finishes his piano suite *Pictures at an Exhibition*, illustrating paintings by his late friend, Victor Hartmann.

1906 'Here I am again with my old friend the Sea; she is always endless and beautiful, the only thing in Nature that shows you how small you are' – the composer of *La Mer*, summering near Dieppe.

1912 Stravinsky calls on Diaghilev at Karlsbad and is commissioned to compose *The Rite of Spring*.

1922 At the first International Festival of Contemporary Music in Salzburg, 'Anton von Webern appears. I never saw an angrier man: he is about 35, dry and thin as though pickled in perennial fury, and erect as a ramrod. It was amusing to see him face up to each of the four executants of his five pieces for string quartet [Op. 5] as if he were going to kill them, then relent, wring his hands bitterly, glare defiance at the audience and rush off stiffly . . .' (*Daily Telegraph*).

1967 'An excessive dose of scenes of violence' is cited by the Argentine armed forces as a reason for banning the opera *Bomarzo* by the country's leading composer, Alberto Ginastera.

1862 Berlioz conducts his opera *Béatrice et Bénédict*, 'a caprice written with the point of a needle', at Baden-Baden.

1913 Rachmaninov dedicates his favourite work, *The Bells*, to the Dutch conductor Willem Mengelberg. In Russian, the Choral symphony is onomatopoeiacally called *Kolokola*.

1928 Unannounced at the end of a Hollywood Bowl concert, before an unsuspecting audience of 15,000, Percy Grainger stages his own wedding to Ella Viola Ström.

1946 Britain enshrines the principle of public funding for music in a Royal Charter granted to the Arts Council to 'preserve and improve standards of performance'. Current annual grants exceed £30m.

1787 *Eine Kleine Nachtmusik* flows from Mozart's pen in Vienna.

1788 A year later, he completes his last symphony, the 'Jupiter'.

1861 London 'makes a gloomy impression on the soul. You never see the sun, and it rains at every step,' moans young Tchaikovsky. He likes the food, though.

1895 The London season of summer Promenade Concerts is founded by Robert Newman and Henry Wood at the Queen's Hall.

1970 Bernd Alois Zimmermann, 52, completing his cantata – 'I turned round and saw all the injustices committed under the sun' – commits suicide in Königsdorf on learning that he is going irreversibly blind.

1848 Chopin finds the Scots 'ugly but good-natured', their cows 'magnificent but inclined to gore people'.

1957 Paul Hindemith examines Kepler's musical theories of planetary motion in an opera, *The Harmony of the World*, at Munich.

1966 Arriving in the US, John Lennon apologises for having claimed that the Beatles are 'more popular than Jesus'.

9 AUGUST

 10 AUGUST

 11 AUGUST

 **12 AUGUST**

 13 AUGUST

 14 AUGUST

1877 Thomas Alva Edison, 30, sketches a cylinder and stylus, scrawls 'Kruesi – make this' in a note to his best mechanic, shouts 'Mary had a little lamb' into the resultant device and invents recording. 'I was never so taken aback in my life,' he recalls of the moment the recranked cylinder gave a graven image of his own voice.

1881 Two months after its opening, the National Theatre in Prague burns down; Smetana, that day, barely escapes being run over by a locomotive.

1928 At 10 p.m. Leos Janáček, 75, perishes of pneumonia caught while searching Hukvaldy for the missing son of his love-object*.

* I have recently pursued this matter exhaustively with scholars in Brno, and regret to report no evidence of consummation.

1936 Paderewski plays Beethoven on the soundtrack of *Moonlight Sonata*. At the film studios, Poland's ex-Premier runs into Winston Churchill, writing a script on his ancestor, Marlborough.

1876 Bayreuth opens with *Das Rheingold*. The inaugural *Ring*, conducted by Hans Richter, is given three times in three weeks. Wagner posts a notice to his singers at the back of the stage and in all dressing rooms: '!! Clarity!! The big notes will look after themselves, the small notes and their text are the main thing. Never address the audience direct . . .'

1900 'This is the best of me; for the rest, I ate, and drank, and slept, and loved and hated, like another: my life was as the vapour and is not; but *this* I saw and knew; this, if anything of mine, is worth your memory' – Elgar signs off *The Dream of Gerontius*.

1912 Jules Massenet, 70, expires in Paris. 'I asked that they should refrain from hanging black draperies on my door, ornaments worn threadbare by use. I expressed the wish that a suitable carriage should take me from Paris, the journey, with my consent, to begin at eight in the morning.'

1814 Rossini's comic *Turk in Italy* opens at La Scala.

1876 *Die Walküre* at Bayreuth. 'Why, of all places, Bayreuth?' demands Eduard Hanslick, leading anti-Wagnerite. 'I doubt that the enjoyment of art is enhanced by being uncomfortably housed for a week, sleeping badly, eating miserably, and after a taxing five or six hours of opera not knowing whether one will find even a small snack.'

Prototype Valkyrie

1892 Composer-pianist Kaikhosru Shapurji Sorabji is born of a Parsee Indian father and Spanish-Sicilian mother at Chingford, Essex. He gives up concerts in the 1920s, stops publishing ten years later and from 1940 forbids performances of his works.

1807 Paganini, on the G-string alone, plays a Napoleon sonata for the Emperor's birthday.

1876 Wagner's *Siegfried* is postponed, owing to the hoarseness of the baritone, Franz Betz.

1951 Artur Schnabel, 69, the first pianist to record Beethoven's 32 sonatas, dies in Switzerland. His credo: 'Man's ability to originate and reproduce is incontestably present in every person.'

1986 'I have gone back to my music of the 1960s,' declares Krzysztof Penderecki of his *Black Mask,* staged at Salzburg.

1876 *Siegfried* sung at Bayreuth.

1936 The Nazi Olympics open in Berlin to Richard Strauss's *Olympic Hymn* and fanfares by other verifiably Aryan composers.

1943 A stray bomb hits La Scala, wrecking the auditorium but sparing the stage.

1944 Strauss watches his last opera, *Die Liebe der Danaë*, in dress rehearsal at Salzburg. It cannot be performed, as Dr Goebbels has closed all theatres in response to the Allied invasion of Europe.

1977 Elvis Presley, 42, ingests a deadly surfeit of drugs in Memphis.

1876 *Götterdämmerung* concludes the inaugural *Ring*.

1880 Ole Bull, powerful violinist, dies exhausted in Bergen having tried and expensively failed to found a Norwegian colony in Pennsylvania and a musical conservatory in Norway.

1914 Elgar, 56, enlists as a special constable in the Hampstead Division, 'to perambulate the streets . . . firmly grasping his truncheon and looking about for German spies and dynamitards' (W. H. Reed).

1933 *Godiva*, yet another Peeping Tom opera, by Ludwig Roselius, is staged in Nazi Nuremberg.

 **15 AUGUST**

 16 AUGUST

 17 AUGUST

18 AUGUST

 19 AUGUST

 20 AUGUST

18 AUGUST

1784 Mozart to his sister, on her wedding:
'The married state will teach you more
Than you had plainly known before
And by experience show to you
What Mother Eve first had to do
So Cain could come into this life.
But all these duties are so light
You will perform them with delight . . .'

1894 Marcel Proust takes a summer break in a country house called Réveillon in Seine-et-Marne with his new love Reynaldo Hahn, 19, Venezuelan-born composer. 'I mean you to be ever-present in my novel, like a god in disguise whom no mortal can recognise,' he tells Reynaldo, prototype of Henri de Réveillon in the novel *Jean Santeuil*.

1942 Erwin Schulhoff, 48, Czech composer of a cantatic setting of the Communist Manifesto, is murdered at the German concentration camp of Wülzburg.

19 AUGUST

1570 Salamone Rossi, 'Ebreo di Mantova', the first Jew to leave his mark on European music, is born in Mantua where he composes for court and synagogue, in Italian and Hebrew, and collaborates with Monteverdi.

1613 Monteverdi becomes maestro di capella at St Mark's, Venice.

1815 Schubert composes five Goethe songs including *Heidenröslein*.

1929 Beside the Venice deathbed of Serge Diaghilev, 57, two acolytes squabble over his legacy. 'Shaken by rage, they rolled on the floor, tearing at each other's clothes, biting one another like wild animals . . . The nurse and I had all we could do to separate them . . . so she could lay out the body' (Misia Sert).

20 AUGUST

1611 Tomás Luis de Victoria, Spanish composer who dominates 16th-century church music alongside his friend Palestrina, dies in Madrid aged 62.

1724 On the 11th Sunday after Trinity, Bach produces the requisite cantata, *Herr Jesu Christ, du höchstes gut*.

1871 Wagner reminisces: 'When I was at Dresden I told Röckel that I hoped to have written all my works before I was 40; I assumed that the sexual urge, with which all productivity is connected, would last until then, Röckel laughed at me and said I might assume that about Rossini, but with me it was quite different' (CWD).

1882 Tchaikovsky's *1812 Overture* thunders forth at the opening of the Cathedral of the Redeemer in the Kremlin. 'The overture will be very loud and noisy but I have written it without affection or enthusiasm, so it will probably have little artistic merit.'

1627 Paris mourns its *'Père de la Musique'*, Jacques Mauduit, 69, a composer who used his influence as personal secretary to Henri IV to save Protestant musicians from the mob.

1750 Handel, on his last trip to Germany, is reported 'terribly hurt' in a coach accident between The Hague and Haarlem.

1772 'Poor scholars' at the Jesuit music school in Munich, notes Dr Burney, 'are obliged frequently to perform in the streets to convince the public, at whose expence they are maintained, of the proficiency they make in their musical studies.'

1912 Elgar finishes *The Music Makers*.
> 'We are the music makers
> And we are the dreamers of dreams,
> Wand'ring by lone sea breakers
> And sitting by desolate streams;
> World losers and world foresakers,
> On whom the pale moon gleams:
> Yet we are the movers and shakers
> Of the world, for ever, it seems.'

1599 Madrigalist Luca Marenzio who 'excelleth all other whosoever, having published more Sets than any other Author', returns from Poland to Rome but finds 'the affection of the Pope so estranged from him that hereupon he took a conceit and died.'

1862 Above the china shop his parents run at Saint Germain-en-Laye, 25 km west of Paris, Achille-Claude Debussy, self-styled *'musicien français'*, is born.

1928 Karlheinz Stockhausen, leader of the post-war avant-garde, is born at Mödrath, a village near Cologne. 'Those who wish to be musicians, following their higher voice, must begin with the simplest exercises of meditation, at first just for oneself: Play a note with the certainty that you have as much time and space as you want ..." They must acquire an awareness about what they are living for, what we are all living for: to achieve a higher life and to let the vibrations of the universe penetrate into our individual human existence' (Stockhausen, letter to the editor of *Art International*, Lugano, 15.6.68).

1782 Leopold Mozart, on his son: 'If he is not actually in want, he becomes indolent and lazy. If he has to bestir himself, then he realises his worth and wants to make his fortune at once.'

1907 Fauré, in the Alps, awaits a visit from Paul Dukas: 'He is not much of a talker; we shall therefore spend a good day together each thinking of his music.'

1945 Leo Borchard, conductor of the re-formed Berlin Philharmonic Orchestra, is shot dead when his driver fails to stop at an American checkpoint.

21 AUGUST

 22 AUGUST

 23 AUGUST

24 AUGUST

 25 AUGUST

 **26 AUGUST**

1687 Michael Wise, 39, composer and Master of the Choristers at St Paul's Cathedral, London, is 'knock'd on the head and kill'd downright by the Night-watch at Salisbury for giving stubborn and refractory language to them on S. Bartholomews day at night' – apparently upon rushing from his house after a row with his wife.

1827 'Best of women, Mother!' – Liszt, 15, in Boulogne, gently breaks the news that his father is dying of typhoid fever.

1972 Sub-titled 'Apply Marxism-Leninism-Mao Zedong Thought in a Living Way to the Problems of the Present', a new version of Cornelius Cardew's *The Great Learning* is given at the BBC Promenade Concerts, London, by the unskilled Scratch Orchestra the composer has founded.

1830 A Brussels performance of Auber's *La Muette de Portici*, depicting an ancient Neapolitan revolution, inspires Belgians to rise up against Dutch rule.

1870 At 8 a.m. on King Ludwig's birthday, Richard and Cosima Wagner are finally wed at a Protestant church in Lucerne.

1900 Friedrich Nietzsche, 55, supremacist philosopher and composer of various choral works, dies insane at Weimar.

1918 Leonard Bernstein breezes in at Lawrence, Massachusetts.

1846 Mendelssohn premieres *Elijah* at Birmingham Town Hall.

1900 After lightning destroys most of the set, Fauré's *Prométhée* is created by 800 performers before 10,000 people in an open amphitheatre at Béziers.

1910 Beside a Dutch canal at Leyden, Sigmund Freud psychoanalyses Gustav Mahler, who is mortally troubled by fear of losing his wife.

1929 George Gershwin makes his debut as a conductor. 'He could hardly contain his enthusiasm,' notes the *New York Times*.

1958 Instead of watching Sir Adrian Boult recording his Ninth Symphony, Ralph Vaughan Williams dies quietly at home. He is 85.

1521 Death of Josquin des Prés, Renaissance composer of whom Martin Luther says, 'Josquin is a unique master of the notes, which must do as he desires; other composers do what the notes dictate.'

1748 Rameau's opera-ballet *Pigmalion* [sic] is seen in Paris.
'Love triumphs, proclaim his victory
This god strives only to fulfil our desires.'

1937 Aaron Copland's *El Salon Mexico* is performed there.

1572 Catholics in Lyon massacre their Protestant neighbours, among them Claude Goudimel, 57, eminent psalm composer.

1733 Pergolesi's two-part comic masterpiece *La serva padrona* (*The Maid as Mistress*) is played between the acts of his remorselessly serious *Il prigionier superbo* (*The Haughty Prisoner*) at Naples.

1850 In Weimar, Franz Liszt conducts *Lohengrin* by Richard Wagner, whom he has helped avoid arrest for insurrection and flee to Switzerland.

1959 Summoning a priest to sanctify his marriage – the original ceremony 26 years earlier was civic – Bohuslav Martinů, exiled Czech composer, dies in Liestal, Switzerland, aged 68.

1859 In a private ceremony, Verdi weds the former singer Giuseppina Strepponi, with whom he has lived for a decade. 'Oh my Verdi I am unworthy of you ... Continue to love me, love me also after death, so that I may present myself to Divine Providence rich with all your love and all your prayers. O my Redeemer!'

1952 John Cage's *4'33"*, a precise period of predetermined inaction, is unplayed by pianist David Tudor at the aptly-named Maverick Concert Hall, Woodstock, New York.

1957 Stravinsky, at the piano of a Venice nightclub, starts composing *Threni*, based on the lamentations of Jeremiah.

 **27 AUGUST**

 28 AUGUST

 29 AUGUST

30 AUGUST

 31 AUGUST

1835 Mendelssohn, 26, arrives in Leipzig as music director. '100 hearts flutter to him the moment he mounts the podium,' writes Schumann.

1933 *The School for Scandal*, an overture by Samuel Barber, 23, after Sheridan's play, is performed by the Philadelphia Orchestra.

1976 In the Vienna apartment where their married life was spent, Helene Berg, 91, dies 40 years after her Alban. It is discovered that his love for a woman in Prague lay behind her refusal to allow the completion of *Lulu*.

1986 Franco Zeffirelli premieres his movie of Verdi's *Otello* at the Vienna State Opera. 'It is not sufficiently borne in mind that in Elizabethan England everybody, especially soldiers, had syphilis' (Zeffirelli/NL).

1848 In a Vienna park frequented by officers, Johann Strauss senior performs his *Radetzky March*, named for the Field Marshal who quashed the Italian uprising. A General in the audience orders him to repeat it four times and the march becomes the anthem of the Austrian army.

1916 For conducting an Italian military band on the newly captured hilltop of Monte Santo, Arturo Toscanini is awarded a medal for bravery.

1928 *The Threepenny Opera* by Bertolt Brecht and Kurt Weill, updating John Gay's *The Beggars' Opera*, opens in Berlin. Mrs Brecht (Helene Weigel) plays the brothel madam; Mrs Weill (Lotte Lenya) sings Jenny.

S·E·P·T·E·M·B·E·R

1785 Mozart dedicates six string quartets to Haydn. 'I send my six sons to you, most celebrated and very dear friend ... From this moment I surrender to you all my rights over them. I entreat you, however, to be indulgent to those faults which may have escaped a father's partial eye.'

1903 Erik Satie writes *Trois Morceaux en Forme de Poire* – 'pear-shaped' because Debussy calls his music shapeless.

1953 A plane crash in the Alps claims the life of violinist Jacques Thibaud, 72, on his way to entertain French troops in Indo-China.

1957 Dennis Brain, 36, outstanding horn player, is killed in a car smash.

1397 Blind Francesco Landini, 62, dies in Florence. 'Francesco, deprived of sight, but with a mind skilled in instrumental music, whom alone Music has set above all others, has left his ashes here, his soul above the stars' (tombstone inscription).

1791 At the climax of an erotic event in a bawdy house in Vine Street, London, Czech composer Franz Kotzwara hangs himself, 'not in jest but in the greatest earnest.'

1929 *Happy End* by Brecht and Weill concludes calamitously when Berlin police rush in to quell riots as Helene Weigel, Brecht's wife, declaims an unscripted Communist manifesto in the third act, inserted by Brecht after he is criticized for lacking political commitment and peddling bourgeois entertainment.

1 SEPTEMBER

2 SEPTEMBER

3 SEPTEMBER

 4 SEPTEMBER

 5 SEPTEMBER

1787 Mozart's doctor dies, aged 29.

1850 K. Freigedank (Freethinker), writing in a weighty music journal, asserts that Jews, notably Mendelssohn and Meyerbeer, are racially incapable of creating European music. 'The Jew speaks the language of the nation in which he dwells but speaks it always as an alien . . . To make poetry in a foreign tongue has always been impossible even to geniuses of the highest order.' The author is revealed to be Richard Wagner.

1912 Arnold Schoenberg's *Five Orchestral Pieces* are premiered by Sir Henry Wood at a London Promenade concert. 'It was like a poem in Tibetan; not one single soul could possibly have understood it at first hearing' (*The Times*).

1914 French symphonist Albéric Magnard falls defending his house on the Marne against advancing German forces. The building is burned, and with it his opera *Bérénice*.

1939 'I had the classic Jungian dream of four men coming out of the corners of the bedroom to . . . and I say: "Let what will be will be." And I wake up. That was exactly the day war broke out. Next day I began *A Child of our Time*' – self-analysis by Sir Michael Tippett.

1824 Anton Bruckner is born at Ansfelden near Linz, Upper Austria, eldest son of the village schoolmaster.

1892 At Aix-en-Provence, Darius Milhaud shares the same birthday. 'I was a well-behaved but rather neurotic child, continually subject to nervous attacks which would be brought on by the slightest thing – a fright, a noise in the dark, a shadow.'

1906 Rimsky-Korsakov completes his autobiography.

1909 Percy Grainger to his mother: 'I just like to be whipped, at any old time, just as I welcome slight burning or any other pain, that is just intense enough to make one say: at last here is a definite feeling.'

1749 Joseph Heidegger, impresario of loss-making Handel operas and lucrative masked balls indicted as 'Nurseries of Lewdness, Extravagance and Immorality,' expires at his Richmond mansion aged 83: 'Of him, it may truly be said, what one hand received from the Rich, the other gave to the Poor' (*General Advertiser*).

1791 Mozart finishes *La clemenza da Tito*, his penultimate opera.

1791 Jakob Liebmann Beer, son of a sugar broker, becomes known as 'the little bear' among the musical stars of Berlin. He renames himself Giacomo Meyerbeer.

1912 John Cage, creator of new sounds on his 'prepared piano' and non-sounds at his most obtuse, springs to life in Los Angeles. 'Try as we may to make a silence, we cannot' (John Cage, *Silence*).

1913 Prokofiev, 22, is the soloist in his second piano concerto at St Petersburg. 'On all sides one hears, "To the devil with this futurist music! My cat can play like that!"' (*St Petersburg Gazette*).

1625 Heinrich Schütz, 40, mourns his wife, Magdalena, at 24 a victim of smallpox. 'Among all the sounds of the harp he neither knew nor heard a lovelier sound or song than the voice of his beloved,' says the pastor. Schütz, contrary to custom, never remarries.

1791 Mozart's *La clemenza de Tito* is staged for the Prague coronation of Leopold II. 'German swinery,' mutters the Empress.

1910 Gloucester Cathedral, packed with an audience of 2,000 for Elgar's *Dream of Gerontius* hears the unknown Ralph Vaughan Williams – '39, magisterial, dark-haired, clear-cut of feature' – conduct his *Fantasia on a Theme by Thomas Tallis*, a 350-year-old idea that struck him while editing the English Hymnal.

1961 'A masterpiece, and by an American composer!' exclaims Stravinsky of Elliott Carter's double concerto.

1962 The mortal odyssey of Hanns Eisler, political composer, ends in East Berlin. Born in Leipzig, taught in Vienna by Schoenberg, he partners Brecht in Berlin, flees from Hitler to Hollywood and from Senator McCarthy to the GDR, where he writes the national anthem.

1741 'We hear from Italy that the famous singer Mrs C-z-ni, is under sentence of death to be beheaded for poisoning her husband' – false report on Handel's star, Francesca Cuzzoni, in the London *Daily Post*.

1819 Jean-Louis Duport – of whose cellism Voltaire said: 'M. Duport, you will make me believe in miracles when I see that you can turn an ox into a nightingale' – dies in Paris aged 80.

Duport

1822 Between 5.30 and 9 p.m., King Pedro I of Brazil composes a national anthem, sung for almost a century, celebrating independence from Portugal. Four years later when Pedro becomes King of Portugal, he transplants his anthem to Lisbon, where it is used for 84 years.

1922 Arthur Bliss conducts at Gloucester his *Colour Symphony* in movements of purple, red, blue and green.

1822 Beethoven is visited by the singers of his Ninth symphony, Henriette Sontag and Karoline Unger. 'Since they wanted by all means to kiss my hands and were really pretty,' he tells his brother, 'I proposed that they kiss my mouth.'

1831 Chopin, in Stuttgart, receives news of the fall of Warsaw to Russian forces: 'The suburbs are destroyed, burned. Johnny and William surely dead on the ramparts ... Mos-

cow rules the world. Oh God, do you exist? You do, and yet you don't take vengeance. How many more Russian crimes do you want? Or – or are you a Russian too!!?'

1894 Hermann von Helmholtz, 73, founder of the study of musical acoustics and inventor of the opthalmoscope, expires in Berlin. 'Helmholtz's head was equal to the size of Bismarck's and rather smaller than Wagner's, both of whom had big

heads. The weight of the brain with blood was 1700 grams, without blood 1400 grams, being about 100 grams heavier than the average human brain' (*Zeitschrift für Psychologie*, 7 March 1895).

1949 'Dying,' confirms Richard Strauss, 85, 'is just as I composed it in *Death and Transfiguration*.'

6 SEPTEMBER

7 SEPTEMBER

8 SEPTEMBER

9 SEPTEMBER

10 SEPTEMBER

11 SEPTEMBER

1796 Haydn's incidental music to *Alfred, King of Angelsey* is converted at Eisenstadt to *Haldane, King of the Danes*.

1907 Some 50,000 people turn out at Bergen for Grieg's cremation. 'There was no cold curiosity, no fighting for places, no stretching of necks to see better. From old man to urchin, all had the same grave expression of face which showed that they felt their loss' (Adolph Brodsky).

1963 Ten pianists led by John Cage attempt Erik Satie's *Véxations*, a 180-note piece to be played 840 times without interruption or variation. The premiere lasts 18 hours 40 minutes but purists say it should have been tackled by one pianist.

1982 Investment publisher Gilbert E. Kaplan, 41, makes his debut as a conductor of Mahler's Second symphony before an international audience of 2700 bank chiefs and ministers of finance at the Lincoln Center, New York. 'I had the feeling they were urging me to fulfil my dream because each of them had a secret ambition he had not attained' (Kaplan/NL).

1772 At the Imperial music library in Vienna, Dr Burney finds 'an immense collection ... in such disorder that their contents are at present almost wholly unknown.'

1941 Christopher Hogwood, 'the Karajan of early music', is born in Nottingham. 'I'm for democracy to the point of anarchy. No one wants ... a bunch of mice playing baroque instruments and a great conductor telling them to do it his way' (Hogwood/NL).

1950 A single-movement Second Symphony by Karl Amadeus Hartmann, whose motto is 'Truth prepared by joy and bound up with sorrow', earns him acclamation as Germany's foremost post-war symphonist.

1733 François Couperin, known as 'Le Grand' to signify his status in a dynasty that bred almost as many musicians as the Bachs, bows out in Paris aged 64. 'Since hardly anyone has composed more than I have ... I hope my family will find in my wallet something to make them regret my passing.'

1827 Berlioz, 23, discovers Shakespeare and his future wife in *Hamlet*, with Harriet Smithson as Ophelia. 'I saw, I understood, I felt ... that I was alive and that I must arise and walk.'

1895 Rachmaninov finishes his First Symphony.

1939 'We're gonna hang out the washing on the Siegfried Line' by Jimmy Kennedy and Michael Carr gives notice of Allied intent.

1764 Jean-Philippe Rameau, 80, French composer and theorist, dies revered yet disliked. 'His heart and soul were in his harpsichord,' says an acquaintance, 'when he shut the lid there was no one at home.'

1835 The bass tuba is patented in Berlin.

1879 'September, with its tender, melancholy colouring, has a special power to fill me with calm and happy feelings' – Tchaikovsky.

1899 Outraged at the Dreyfus Affair, Grieg refuses to conduct in France. 'Like all outsiders, I am indignant at the contempt for justice shown in your country, and am therefore unable to enter into relations with the French public.'

1910 Mahler enjoys his greatest triumph at the Munich premiere of his massive Eighth, the 'Symphony of a Thousand'. 'The experience was indescribable. Indescribable too the demonstration that followed. The whole audience [of 3000] surged towards the platform ...' (Alma Mahler).

1870 Gounod flees war-stricken France to settle in England.

1894 Emmanuel Chabrier, 53, composer, art-fancier and civil servant, dies in Paris of the effects of syphilis. His personal effects include 6 Renoirs, 8 Monets, 2 Sisleys, 2 Fantin-Latours and 11 Manets.

1899 'A wave of vulgar, filthy and suggestive music has inundated the land' – the *Musical Courier*

reports the arrival of ragtime.

1934 On Schoenberg's birthday, his disciple Webern dedicates a symmetrical concerto (Op. 24) whose notes mirror the Latin palindrome:

```
S A T O R
A R E P O
T E N E T
O P E R A
R O T A S
```
(Arepo the sower controls the work), each line of which can be read back-

wards, vertically and horizontally.

1956 'MURDER IN THE CATHEDRAL' headlines *Time* magazine as Igor Stravinsky conducts in St Mark's, by permission of Cardinal Roncalli of Venice (later Pope John XIII), the first performance of *Canticum Sacram ad Honorem Sancti Marci Nominis*.

1814 'The Star-Spangled Banner' adopted as US national anthem in 1931, is written aboard a British frigate by Francis Scott Key of Baltimore, while negotiating the release of a captured friend and witnessing the bombing of Fort McHenry. 'At early dawn his eye was again greeted by the proudly waving flag of his country.'

1917 Opening the State Theatre in Petrograd between two revolutions, conductor Nikolai Malko has to give nine performances of the *Marseillaise* before the concert can proceed.

1936 A typewriter of musical notation is patented in Berlin.

1960 Aged 54, Dmitri Shostakovich joins the Communist Party of the USSR. 'It was made clear to him that if he did not become a member, his music would not be played' (Rotislav Dubinsky/NL).

12 SEPTEMBER

13 SEPTEMBER

14 SEPTEMBER

15 SEPTEMBER

 16 SEPTEMBER

 17 SEPTEMBER

1819 Beethoven's *Hammerklavier* sonata, Op. 106, is published. It was written, he says, 'almost for the sake of bread alone'.

1849 Bruckner's first significant work, a Requiem in D minor in memory of a family friend who had bequeathed him a Bösendorfer grand piano, is sung at St Florian's monastery, near Linz, where the 25-year-old composer is probationary organist.

1894 On his 18th birthday in Hamburg, Bruno Walter makes his debut as conductor in Flotow's incidental music to Shakespeare's *A Winter's Tale*.

1945 Smoking a post-supper cigar at Mittersill near Salzburg, Anton von Webern, 62, is accidentally shot dead by an American soldier arriving to arrest his black-marketeer son-in-law.

1787 Haydn writes the 'Frog' quartet, so nicknamed for its croaky finale.

1800 Adrien Boieldieu, 25, scoring an instant hit with *The Caliph of Baghdad*, is accosted in the lobby by Luigi Cherubini. '*Malheureux*,' declares the Italian, 'are you not ashamed of such undeserved success?' Boieldieu meekly enrols as his pupil.

1966 The $46m Metropolitan Opera House at Lincoln Center opens with *Antony and Cleopatra* by Samuel Barber, with libretto and lavish production by Franco Zeffirelli. 'Artifice masquerading with great flourish as art,' says the *New York Times*.

1977 Felled by a heart attack as she rises in the morning to go to the bathroom, Maria Callas, 53, dies in Paris.

1179 Hildegard of Bingen, 'the Sybil of the Rhine', composer of monophonic songs and scientific treatises, seer of visions, intimate of emperors and popes, surrenders her 81-year-old soul: 'It pleased a King to raise a small feather from the ground and he commanded it to fly. The feather flew, not because of anything in itself but because the air bore it along. Thus am I . . .'

1762 Francesco Geminiani, 74, violinist and composer, collapses in Dublin on finding that his maid has made off with the only copy of his unpublished manual of violin playing.

1901 'If destiny, through some devil's intrigue, were to force me to live in Glasgow, I should give up music and become an umbrella maker' – Ferruccio Busoni, letter to his wife.

1931 *A Song of Summer*, 'dictated' by blind, paralysed Delius to a volunteer copyist, Eric Fenby, is performed at the Proms, the composer listening at home in France to a wireless relay. 'It's a good piece, lad,' he pronounces.

1837 'The interview with your father was terrible. Such coldness, such malice, such distraction, such contradictions – he has a new way of destroying someone, he thrusts the knife into your heart up to the hilt ... I feel so dead, so humiliated, that I can barely grasp one beautiful, pleasant thought; even your picture eludes me, I can hardly remember your eyes ... To be forbidden even to see you!' writes despairing Schumann to his unattained Clara.

1857 'On this day, at this hour, I was born again.' Wagner sends his *Tristan* poem to the married woman who inspired it, Mathilde Wesendonck.

1918 English composer Ernest Farrar, 33, is killed on the Somme. His pupil, Gerald Finzi, becomes an ardent pacifist.

1918 Prokofiev arrives in America, a refugee from revolution.

1738 'Mr Handel's head is more full of maggots than ever' – Charles Jennens, librettist of *Messiah*.

1869 Wagner and Nietzsche squabble over food. The philosopher says it is morally wrong to eat meat. The composer retorts that man's whole existence is a compromise, which can only be expiated by producing some good: to do good, one needs good nourishment.

Heady Handel

1908 Mahler's Seventh symphony is 'scarcely understood' in Prague.

1917 Arnold Schoenberg, 43, joins the Austrian army. 'Aren't you the notorious modernist composer?' he is quizzed by comrades-in-arms. 'Somebody had to be,' replies Schoenberg, 'and since no one else wanted to, I took it on myself.'

1460 The death of Gilles Binchois, 60-ish, Franco-Flemish composer, is mourned in music by his colleagues Dufay and Ockeghem.

1823 'He was a kleptomaniac ... to this he added a reckless extravagance in money matters that amounted to criminality ... His respect for his art, never too great, was destroyed by the quantity of worthless music that he wrote hastily to meet temporary difficulties, and he not unfrequently stooped to expedients still more unworthy' – Daniel Steibelt, 58, composer of the first piano concerto with a choral finale, dies friendless in St Petersburg.

1957 Sibelius, 91, fades out at Järvenpää, after 33 years of unexplained musical quietude.

18 SEPTEMBER

19 SEPTEMBER

20 SEPTEMBER

21 SEPTEMBER

  22 SEPTEMBER

  23 SEPTEMBER

1874 Gustav Holst is born at Cheltenham, 'a delicate child, short-sighted and asthmatic'.

1897 Hugo Wolf, proclaiming himself director of the Vienna Opera, is gently shepherded into a lunatic asylum.

1899 Mahler acquires some 3000 square metres of land beside the Wörthersee to build the summer home where he composes Symphonies 5 to 8.

1899 Francis Barraud's painting of a dog called Nipper listening to a record player, is bought from the artist for £100 by the Gramophone Company, re-titled 'His Master's Voice' and registered as a trade mark.

1825 Giacomo Meyerbeer opens his Paris career with *The Crusader in Egypt*, the last major opera to contain a *castrato* role.

1830 Chopin, 20, summons musical Warsaw to his home for a dress rehearsal of the newly-finished E minor Concerto.

1869 At King Ludwig's orders and against Wagner's wishes, *Das Rheingold* is produced in Munich. 'Keep your hands off my score!' Wagner bludgeons the conductor, Franz Wüllner; to no avail.

1888 Schubert's remains, exhumed at Währing, are fingered fondly by the sentimental Anton Bruckner before removal to Vienna's new central cemetery.

1985 For the D. H. Lawrence centenary, a musical suite by fellow-novelist Anthony Burgess is played in his native Nottingham.

1835 Vincenzo Bellini, 33, dies at Puteaux, outside Paris. Rossini reports: 'A dysentery which increased over a period of 15 days to the point of inflammation, had defeated all the resources of the medical profession. I am inconsolable . . . all Paris mourns . . . tell Bellini's relatives and friends that the only consolation left to me is to devote all my care to honouring him as friend, fellow-countryman and artist.'

1836 Maria Malibran, 28, magnificent mezzo, collapses at Manchester after unwisely duetting with a rival, Maria Caradori Allen. 'If I sing again,' she warns before her last encore, 'it will kill me.'

1886 Bruckner is received in audience by the Emperor Franz Joseph. 'Would Your Majesty be kind enough,' he begs, 'to tell Mr Hanslick not to write such bad criticisms of my work?'

1986 Amsterdam joins the opera world with an £85m Muziektheater. Massed police protect the opening from environmental and anti-nuclear protesters.

1645 In the siege of Chester during the English Civil War, 'Gentle Willy' Lawes, composer, is caught fatally in crossfire.

1891 Wounded by sniggers about her expanding figure, Marie Wilt, Vienna's first Aïda, throws herself out of a window.

1914 Composer Andrzej Panufnik draws breath in Warsaw. 'The year 1914 was a bad time to be born in Poland. Until I was 6 or 7 there was little food to be had, even if you had money. The Second War broke at the height of my creative powers. Then in 1949 came the suffocation of artists.'

1947 The Committee on Un-American Activities interrogates composer Hanns Eisler: 'Are you now, or have you ever been a communist?' Eisler replies: I am not now a communist. I remember I made, when I was a young man, in 1926, an application for the German Communist Party, but I found out very quickly that I couldn't combine my artistic activities with the demands of any political party, so I dropped out.'

1849 With 20 bars written of a *Radetzky Banquet March*, Op. 252, Johann Strauss the elder is a victim of meningitis arising from scarlet fever caught from a daughter of his common-law wife, who flees their home.

1890 Tchaikovsky is told by Nadezhda von Meck that she can no longer afford to support him.

1903 After living together for six years, Delius weds the painter Jelka Rosen. 'No artist should ever marry . . . if you ever do have to marry, marry a girl who is more in love with your art than with you' (Delius to Eric Fenby).

1906 Dmitri Shostakovich is born in St Petersburg. His chemist father is descended from Polish insurrectionists; his mother is a pianist.

1907 Sibelius conducts his Third Symphony in Helsingfors amid such excitement that his portrait is in all shop windows and a cigar is named after him.

1782 The original *Barber of Seville*, Paisiello's, premieres in St Petersburg and soon sweeps Europe.

1892 Dvořák arrives in America just after 6 p.m.

1898 The Gershwins, Lower East Side immigrants from St Petersburg, beget a boy, Jacob, who calls himself George.

1938 'September Song' is sung at Hartford, Connecticut, as Kurt Weill's *Knickerbocker Holiday* opens out of town.

1945 At New York's West Side hospital, Béla Bartók, 64, loses his battle with leukaemia. 'My father produced music virtually up to the last minute. He was finishing the third piano concerto for my mother when the doctors came. He begged them to let him remain at home one more day but they

were adamant. A week later he died anyway. The last 17 bars had to be scored by Tibor Serly' (Peter Bartók/NL).

1957 Leonard Bernstein's *West Side Story* opens at the Winter Garden, New York.

 **24 SEPTEMBER**

 25 SEPTEMBER

 **26 SEPTEMBER**

27 SEPTEMBER

 28 SEPTEMBER

 29 SEPTEMBER

1827 Schubert lets a friend hear his last three sonatas.

1921 Arnold Schoenberg begins his Wind Serenade, Op. 24, the first 12-note composition. He tells a pupil: 'I have made a discovery that will ensure the superiority of German music for the next 100 years.'

Schubert

1934 Vaughan Williams conducts his famed Fantasia on 'Greensleeves' from the opera *Sir John in Love.*

1956 Chickenpox caught at Cheltenham kills Gerald Finzi, 55, lyrical English composer.

1886 At his wedding, the Belgian violinist Eugène Ysaÿe receives a surprise gift from his compatriot César Franck: the violin sonata in A major.

1918 Stravinsky's *L'Histoire du Soldat*, to C. F. Ramuz's tale of a soldier who surrenders his violin and his soul, is conducted in Lausanne by Ernest Ansermet. 'My uninterrupted collaboration with Ramuz . . . helped me to bear the difficult times through which I was living, sickened and, as a patriot, desperately humiliated as I was by the monstrous [Soviet–German] Peace of Brest-Litovsk' (Stravinsky, *Autobiography*).

1947 *The Great Friendship* by an insignificant Georgian, Vano Muradeli, written for the 30th anniversary of the Red Revolution, is staged in Stalino and a dozen other cities, provoking Stalin to launch his second persecution of the USSR's finest composers.

1789 Mozart writes his clarinet quintet.

1829 Paganini visits Goethe.

1873 A construction worker falls to his death from the top scaffold of Wagner's theatre in Bayreuth.

1918 Hearing that Gustav Holst has been drafted to serve in the Middle East, wealthy composer Balfour Gardiner gives him the Queen's Hall, orchestra and chorus for a morning – so that Adrian Boult can rehearse and privately perform for the first time *The Planets.*

1755 Church composer Francesco Durante, 71, dies at Naples 'of a diarrhoea brought on by a feed of melons'.

1791 *The Magic Flute* opens at the Theater an der Wien. Mozart plays the glockenspiel at an early performance, throwing Papageno off his lines.

1853 Brahms, 20, visits Robert and Clara Schumann in Düsseldorf. Schumann publicly proclaims him 'a Chosen One', stifling the shy young man for years.

The Magic Flute

1919 Leos Janáček, inaugurating the Conservatoire in Brno: 'Who would like to teach a robin to sing? Who would like to teach someone to be a composer? A composer is born. It can't be taught.'

1935 In Boston, the curtain rises on *Porgy and Bess*.

1 OCTOBER

2 OCTOBER

O · C · T · O · B · E · R

---

1 OCTOBER

1667 'To White Hall; and there in the Boarded Gallery did hear the musick with which the King is presented this night by Monsieur Grebus, the master of his music ... But, God forgive me! I never was so little pleased with a consort of musick in my life. The manner of setting the words and repeating them out of order and that with a number of voices, makes me sick ...' – Samuel Pepys.

1733 Days after his 50th birthday, Rameau produces his first opera *Hippolyte et Aricie*. For the next 30 years he writes only for the stage.

1772 Frederick the Great plays his flute for Dr Burney. 'His majesty executed the solo parts with great precision, his embouchure was clear and even, and his finger brilliant, and his taste pure and simple ... It is easy to discover that these concertos were composed at a time when he did not so frequently require an opportunity of breathing ...'

---

2 OCTOBER

1849 A week after his father's demise, Johann Strauss the younger, 24, takes over his orchestra in a programme ending with the *Radetzky March*. He quells mutiny among the musicians and mutterings in the audience by telling the *Wiener Zeitung* that he is the sole supporter of his father's poor orphans. 'I shall show myself worthy of him,' he adds.

1852 'Pianos and guitars groan with it night and day ... The street organs grind it out at every hour ... The chamber maid sweeps and dusts to the measured cadence of 'Old Folks at Home'; the butcher's boy treats you to a strain or two of it as he hands in the steaks for dinner; the milkman mixes it up strangely with the harsh ding-dong accompaniment of his tireless bell' (*Dwight's Journal of Music*, Boston).

1913 Simultaneous premieres of four English masterpieces: *On Hearing the first Cuckoo in Spring* and *Summer Night on the River* by Delius are played in Leipzig, Elgar directs his symphonic poem *Falstaff* at the Leeds Festival, where Nikisch conducts George Butterworth's rhapsody, *A Shropshire Lad*.

205

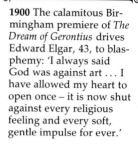

1853 George Onslow, composer of English origin (his father was an MP exiled by a homosexual scandal), dies in France. His first brush with mortality – a bullet grazed his scalp while out hunting – gave rise to his *Ball Quintet*, Op. 38.

1900 The calamitous Birmingham premiere of *The Dream of Gerontius* drives Edward Elgar, 43, to blasphemy: 'I always said God was against art ... I have allowed my heart to open once – it is now shut against every religious feeling and every soft, gentle impulse for ever.'

1929 Paul Hindemith is the soloist in Walton's Viola Concerto.

1936 Minimalist Stephen Michael (Steve) Reich is born in New York to songwriter June Sillman ('Love is a Simple Thing'), soon to divorce her lawyer husband. 'I was', he reflects, 'their only joint venture.'

1953 Arnold Bax, who dreads reaching the age of 70, falls short of it by one month and five days.

1530 'There are undoubtedly many seeds of good virtue in souls who like music ... and the devil flees from the sound of music almost as he flees from the word of theology ...' – Martin Luther to the Catholic composer Ludwig Senfl.

1910 *The Snowman* by 13-year-old Erich Wolfgang Korngold is seen at the Vienna Opera. The composer is the son of Austria's foremost music critic.

1962 EMI issue The Beatles' first recording, *Love Me Do* coupled with *P.S., I Love You*. It reaches number 17 in the hit parade.

1970 Janis Joplin, 27, overdoses on heroin.

1982 Glenn Gould, 50, non-performing Canadian pianist (he gave up concerts in 1964), is felled by a stroke.

1762 In Vienna, Gluck conducts *Orfeo ed Euridice*, the opera that inaugurates his stylistic revolution.

1789 Parisians marching on Versailles to seize the King give voice to the revolutionary chant '*Ça ira!*' (That will succeed!); the tune is supplied by one Bécourt, a player in the royal opera orchestra.

1823 Weber calls on Beethoven at Baden. 'We all felt strangely moved when entering the great man's poor desolate-looking room; everything in the most appalling disorder – music, money, clothing on the floor, the bed unmade, broken coffee-cups upon the table, the open pianoforte with scarcely any strings left and thickly covered with dust, while he himself was wrapped in a shabby old dressing-gown' (Julius Benedict).

1880 Jacques Offenbach, entertainer of the Second Empire, dies in Paris aged 61.

3 OCTOBER

 4 OCTOBER

 5 OCTOBER

6 OCTOBER

7 OCTOBER

8 OCTOBER

1600 At the wedding of Henri IV of France to Maria de Medici in Florence, Jacopo Peri sings the role of Orpheus in his *Euridice*, the earliest surviving opera (his *Dafne* of 1597 is lost).

1802 'O my fellow men who consider me or describe me as unfriendly, stubborn or even misanthropic, how greatly do you wrong me. For you do not know the secret reason that makes me appear so' – Beethoven, in his Heiligenstadt Testament, confesses to his brothers the agonies of encroaching deafness.

1820 Nightingale Jenny Lind is born illegitimate in Stockholm.

1909 Clara Clemens, Mark Twain's soprano daughter, marries Ossip Gabrilowitsch, Russian-born pianist and conductor.

1927 *The Jazz Singer*, the earliest movie with integral speech and song, opens in New York.

1828 Goethe condemns Rossini's *Moses*: 'There ought to be no praying on the stage.'

1909 Rimsky-Korsakov's last opera, *The Golden Cockerel*, opens in Moscow, gaining fame in Paris five years later as a Diaghilev ballet.

1923 Adolf Hitler, 33 days before launching his Beerhall Putsch in Munich, visits Bayreuth as a guest of the Wagners. 'He looked rather common in Bavarian leather breeches, short woollen socks, a red and blue checked shirt and a short blue jacket that bagged about his unpadded skeleton' (Friedelind Wagner).

1932 'Nothing so electrifying has been heard in a London concert room for years' – Ernest Newman, on the inaugural performance of Beecham's London Philharmonic Orchestra.

1585 Heinrich Schütz, the first internationally known German composer, is born at Köstritz in Saxony.

1910 Arnold Schoenberg's paintings are exhibited in Vienna; Mahler, anonymously, buys one.

1930 Toru Takemitsu, self-taught Japanese composer, emerges in Tokyo. 'My music is very much influenced from gardens and, at the same time, scroll paintings. My musical form, construction, is very like, yes, a scroll.'

1962 After an absence of 48 years, Igor Stravinsky conducts two concerts in his native Leningrad. The audience is officially told that Stravinsky 'always remained a Russian artist spreading the glory of Russian art.'

1813 The date Verdi recognises as his birthday. 'Alas! Born poor in a poor village, I had no way to gain an education. They put a miserable spinet under my hands, and some time later I began to write notes ... notes upon notes. That is all.'

1826 Rossini triumphs with *Le Siège de Corinthe*, his first French opera.

1835 Camille Saint-Saëns is born in Paris.

Saint-Saëns

1891 George Bernard Shaw, at a mighty premiere: 'Dvořák's *Requiem* bored Birmingham so desperately that it was unanimously voted a work of extraordinary depth and impressiveness, which verdict I record with a hollow laugh and allow the subject to drop by its own portentous weight.'

1802 'To be read and executed after my death ... Oh Providence – do but grant me one day of pure joy – For so long now the inner echo of real joy has been unknown to me – Oh when – oh when Almighty God – shall I be able to hear and feel this echo again in the temple of nature and mankind – Never? – no! – Oh, that would be too hard' – Beethoven's postscript to the Heiligenstadt Testament, found in his papers at his death 25 years later.

1813 Verdi's date of birth, as recorded by the Provost of Le Roncole village in the province of Parma, and accepted by most authorities.

1853 Richard Wagner, 40, is introduced by Liszt to his 15-year-old daughter, Cosima. They celebrate this day ever after.

1891 The music of Delius is first heard in public at an Oslo concert.

1906 Son of a Sicilian labourer, composer Paul Creston is born in New York as Giuseppe Gutoveggio but changes his name on getting married.

1919 After *Die Frau ohne Schatten* at the Vienna State Opera, Pauline Strauss snubs her husband in the foyer.

1939 Lenin is the hero of *During the Storm*, an opera by Tikhon Khrennikov, 26, soon to become Stalin's hatchet-man at the Union of Soviet Composers.

1947 Leningrad hears Prokofiev's Sixth symphony.

1968 Luciano Berio catches the international ear with his *Sinfonia*, a collage of Brazilian anthropology, Mahler, Beckett, Joyce and Parisian student slogans, performed by the Swingle Singers and the New York Philharmonic Orchestra.

1985 Claus Helmut Drese takes over the directorship of the Vienna State Opera in partnership with Claudio Abbado.

Verdi's birthplace

10 OCTOBER

11 OCTOBER

 12 OCTOBER

 13 OCTOBER

1727 Handel's anthem *Zadok the Priest* is sung at the coronation of King George II at Westminster Abbey, and at every British coronation since.

1896 After a morning working on the finale of his Ninth symphony, Anton Bruckner, 74, dies at his home in the gatekeeper's lodge of Belvedere Palace, Vienna.

1952 On the day he finishes the opera *War and Peace*, Prokofiev's Seventh and last symphony is performed in Moscow.

1963 Within hours of one another in Paris, tragic chanteuse Edith Piaf, 47, and the 74-year-old poet Jean Cocteau, wordsmith to *Les Six* and Stravinsky's *Oedipus Rex* – depart this fleshly life.

1613 Monteverdi reports that he has been robbed by highwaymen on his way to Venice: 'When they had thoroughly ransacked all our belongings, [one] ... came over to me and ordered me to undress so that he could see if I had any more money. When I declared I had none, he went over to my maidservant and would have submitted her to the same treatment but she resisted with many prayers, entreaties and tears ...'

1910 On his 38th birthday, Vaughan Williams conducts his First symphony at Leeds: 'big stuff – with some impertinences,' says Sir Hubert Parry.

1935 Luciano Pavarotti, large white tenor with handkerchief to match, is born at Modena.

1986 *Love, Death and Tango*, chamber opera by Wilhelm Dieter Siebert, is 'a complete success in every way' at Cassel.

1700 'The score of the musick for the *Fairy Queen* set by the late Mr Henry Purcell, and belonging to the Patentees of the Theatre Royal in Covent Garden, London, being lost by his death, whosoever brings the said score or a copy thereof, to Mr Zackary Baggs, Treasurer of the said Theatre, shall have 20 guineas reward' – advertisement in the *London Gazette*.

1885 Bruckner begs the Vienna Philharmonic Orchestra not to play his Seventh Symphony. 'This request is prompted solely by the depressing local situation concerning leading representatives of the Press which could only be detrimental to the success I am beginning to enjoy in Germany.'

1904 Lily Debussy shoots herself non-fatally when the composer leaves her for Emma Bardac.

1984 Pierre Boulez conducts his third version of *Répons*, employing the 4X computer, capable of 200 million musical operations per second. 'Music must be a pleasure with many layers, some superficially pleasant, others more profound. The epitome of a work of art, for me, is a labyrinth in which you can lose yourself' (Boulez/NL).

1921 'Zemlinsky can wait,' declares Arnold Schoenberg on his unsung brother-in-law's 50th birthday.

1924 Fauré, 79 and ailing, tells his wife that he is returning to Paris where 'I shall spend a little of each day giving you, for consignment to the *flames*, all my sketches, all my rough drafts, all the bits and pieces of which I want *nothing to survive me.'*

1924 Schoenberg's opera *Die Glückliche Hand*, about an artist's search for happiness, is produced in Vienna.

1933 Zemlinsky's *The Chalk Circle* is staged in Zurich.

1977 Out golfing near Madrid, crooner Bing Crosby collapses, aged 74.

1981 Three players in the Israel Philharmonic Orchestra walk out and the Tel Aviv audience erupts as Zubin Mehta unannouncedly conducts the *Tristan* prelude, flouting a 42-year ban on Wagner.

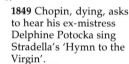

1815 Schubert, 18, in the space of a single day, writes eight songs including *'An die Geliebte'* and *'Wiegenlied'*.

1844 At Dommayer's Garden Restaurant, Vienna, Johann Strauss II on his debut as bandmaster has to repeat his waltz *Sinngedichte* 19 times – a world record.

1849 Chopin, dying, asks to hear his ex-mistress Delphine Potocka sing Stradella's 'Hymn to the Virgin'.

1900 The Boston Symphony Orchestra enters the perfect acoustic of Symphony Hall; the architect is Wallace Sabine.

1905 *La Mer*, Debussy's impression of the English Channel, receives a stormy reception in Paris from critics scandalised by the composer's domestic upheavals.

1963 The polygonic 2200-seat Berlin Philharmonie (architect: Hans Scharoun) featuring 136 ceiling-hung Helmholtz resonators to reflect the sound, opens with Karajan conducting Beethoven's Ninth symphony.

1590 Don Carlo Gesualdo, Prince of Venosa, returns home to find his wife asleep beside her lover, the Duke of Andria. 'Shaking off the dejection into which this miserable spectacle had plunged him, he slew [them] with innumerable dagger thrusts ... The lady's wounds were all in the belly, and more particularly in those parts which she ought to have kept honest; and the Duke was wounded even more grievously.' In the view of

one scholar: 'It was not until Gesualdo gave up murder that he seriously took to composing.'

1750 Lutenist Silvius Leopold Weiss, 64, dies intact at Dresden, 28 years after a French rival tried unsuccessfully to bite off his thumb.

1814 Schubert's first Mass is sung at the Lichtental parish church, his first love, Therese Grob, singing the soprano part.

1909 Composer Percy Grainger, in a state of severe sexual confusion, pulls out all his pubic hair.

 **14 OCTOBER**

 15 OCTOBER

 16 OCTOBER

17 OCTOBER

18 OCTOBER

19 OCTOBER

1849 Chopin, 39, expires in Paris of consumption. 'As this cough will choke me, I beg you to have my body opened so that I am not buried alive' (his last written words).

1891 Declaring that he 'would go to Hell if they gave me a permanent orchestra', conductor Theodore Thomas heads for Illinois to launch the Chicago Symphony Orchestra.

Gounod's last lines

1893 At 6.25 a.m. after two days in a coma, during which he clutched a crucifix all the while, Charles Gounod, 75, breathes his last.

1967 *Hair*, a musical spectacle of psychedelia, four-letter expletives and unfettered nudity, opens in New York.

1752 A philosopher's opera, *Le devin du village* by Jean-Jacques Rousseau, is staged at the court of Louis XV.

1848 Verdi tells the Italian revolutionary leader, Giuseppe Mazzini. 'I am sending you a hymn ... I have tried to be as popular and simple as is possible for me. Make of it what you like, burn it if you find it unworthy ... May this hymn, amid the music of cannon, be sung soon on the plains of Lombardy.'

1887 Brahms' Double Concerto, his last orchestral work, is performed at Cologne.

1904 Mahler directs his Fifth symphony at Cologne, complaining that 'conductors for the next 50 years will all take [the Scherzo] too fast and make nonsense of it.'

1845 Wagner conducts *Tannhäuser* at Dresden.

1886 Tchaikovsky, in his diary: 'Played over the music of that scoundrel Brahms. What a giftless bastard!'

1922 Ravel's orchestration of Mussorgsky's *Pictures at an Exhibition* is conducted in Paris by Serge Koussevitsky who pays him 10,000 francs for it.

1870 Death of Michael William Balfe, 62, Irishman who wrote operas for La Scala and Covent Garden and scored a considerable hit with *The Bohemian Girl*.

1874 Charles Edward Ives is born at Danbury, Connecticut. 'My father ... had a reverence, a devotion and a talent for music ... His interest lay not only in what had been done but in what might be done ...'

1914 Adelina Patti, aged 71, sings at the Royal Albert Hall in aid of the Red Cross.

1973 After 16 years and a cost of 102 million Australian dollars, the Sydney Opera House is opened by Queen Elizabeth II.

1974 Hans-Werner Henze's semi-electronic *Tristan* and Elliott Carter's *Brass Quintet* are premiered in London on the same day.

1784 In Paris, *Richard Coeur de Lion*, Grétry's opera on the fable of the captured English king and his faithful minstrel, presages Wagner's use of the leitmotiv.

1838 Donizetti rents a Paris apartment in the same house as Adolphe Adam (*Giselle*), who notes that 'he worked without a piano and wrote without pause; you could not believe he was composing, until you noticed the absence of any kind of rough copy.'

1858 Offenbach's *Orpheus in the Underworld* makes the can-can the rage of the Second Empire.

1926 Nielsen renounces the symphony, with a flute concerto played in Paris. 'The flute cannot belie its true nature,' he writes.

1764 Returning home after dark Jean-Marie Leclair, 67, composer and violinist, is stabbed to death on his Paris doorstep. Police suspect his nephew, Guillaume-François Vial, a young violinist attached to Leclair's estranged wife/publisher, but no charges are brought.

1811 Franz Liszt is born in Raiding, Hungary, an only child.

Boy Liszt

1891 A baby is christened Fidelio Finke in Josefsthal, Bohemia. He fulfills parental ambitions by becoming a composer.

1930 The BBC Symphony Orchestra assembles. 'In the very sonority of "God Save the King" ... London now possessed the material of a first-class orchestra' (*Morning Post*).

1973 Pablo Casals draws his last bow in Puerto Rico, aged 96.

20 OCTOBER

21 OCTOBER

 22 OCTOBER

23 OCTOBER

24 OCTOBER

25 OCTOBER

1897 Scriabin, 25, plays his own piano concerto in Odessa.

1923 Ned Rorem, art-song composer and epigrammatist – 'Music is the sole art which evokes nostalgia for the future' – hails from Richmond, Indiana.

1931 Stravinsky in Berlin conducts his Violin Concerto, with Samuel Dushkin as soloist. 'Possibly the most wilful, insincere and meretricious score that the creator of *Petrushka* and *Le Sacre* has promulgated in years,' notes the *New York Times*.

1932 Leaving the Charlottenburg Opera House in Berlin where she has just sung Brünnhilde, soprano Gertrud Bindernagel is shot dead by her jealous banker husband, Wilhelm Hintze.

1690 The poet Dryden discovers Henry Purcell, 'in whose Person we have at length found an *Englishman* equal with the best abroad.'

1818 Mendelssohn, 9, makes his concert debut in Berlin.

1850 Hours before his inauguration as music director in Düsseldorf, Schumann finishes his Cello Concerto in A minor, Op. 129.

1920 Milhaud's *Suite symphonique* is played in Paris. 'With the fugue, an indescribable tumult broke out, a real battle in the course of which M. Franck, the organist from the Temple de la Victoire, had his face slapped by Durey ... I had the satisfaction of seeing M. Brancour, the critic of *Le Menestrel* thrown out by two policemen ... My parents were horrified' (Milhaud, *Notes without music*).

1925 Luciano Berio is born at Oneglia on the Italian Riviera. Damage to a hand in 1944 wrecks his ambition to be a concert pianist.

1962 *0'00"*, the shortest piece of music ever written, is completed by John Cage in Tokyo. The score runs to four pages.

1823 Weber's *Euryanthe* triumphs in Vienna. '100 pens were ready, 1000 fists were clenched, to do battle in the cause of German art' (Weber's son).

1875 In Boston, Hans von Bülow has to repeat the entire finale when he premieres Tchaikovsky's first piano concerto, rejected in Russia.

Profound Brahms

1878 'Mussorgsky is such a physical wreck that he could hardly become more of a corpse' – Balakirev, on his protégé.

1885 Brahms' Fourth symphony, played at Meiningen, is almost too deep for his greatest admirer. 'It is like a dark well,' proclaims Eduard Hanslick, 'the longer we gaze into it, the more brightly the stars shine back.'

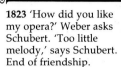

1685 Domenico Scarlatti, pianistic innovator, is born in Naples to opera composer Alessandro. 'Scarlatti was, more than all else, the Neapolitan. He had, even, the alert nerves of someone who is used to traffic. No one who has passed his life in the country could have written the music of Scarlatti' (Sacheverell Sitwell).

1823 'How did you like my opera?' Weber asks Schubert. 'Too little melody,' says Schubert. End of friendship.

1871 'R. reads me an alteration he has made in Brünnhilde's last words: I beg him to leave it as it was, and he agrees, saying that the new version comes too close to literary drama,' writes Cosima Wagner.

1879 Édouard Lalo's *Rhapsodie norvégienne* fails to strike the same chord as his *Symphonie espagnole*.

1678

'Aged 86
October 27
In anno 78
he went to heaven'

Tombstone inscription in Kimberley, Norfolk, for John Jenkins, English composer.

1782 Niccolò Paganini is born in Genoa. 'When I was 5½ my father, a commercial broker, taught me the mandolin. About this time the Saviour appeared to my mother in a dream, bidding her to request some favour, and she asked that her son might become a great violinist; which wish was granted her' (*Autobiography*; dictated at 3.00 a.m., 28 February, 1828).

1917 Jascha Heifetz, 16, makes his US debut at Carnegie Hall in a recital attended by leading virtuosi. 'Phew, it's hot in here!' exclaims Mischa Elman to keyboard wizard Leopold Godowsky. 'Not,' retorts Godowsky famously, 'for pianists.'

1787 At the dress rehearsal of *Don Giovanni*, Mozart, dissatisfied with Zerlina's cries to be saved from the Don, creeps up behind her and, at the appropriate moment, pinches her sharply on the arm. 'Admirable!' he exclaims at her shriek. 'Mind you scream like that on the night.'

1893 Tchaikovsky conducts his Sixth symphony to a St Petersburg audience bewildered by the slow finale. His brother calls it *Pathétique*.

1917 Mischa Elman telephones the young Heifetz to congratulate him on his debut. 'I always have success,' is the icy reply.

1949 Flying to the United States, violinist Ginette Neveu, 30, and her pianist brother Jean perish in an air disaster.

26 OCTOBER

27 OCTOBER

28 OCTOBER

29 OCTOBER

 30 OCTOBER

 31 OCTOBER

1787 Hours before *Don Giovanni*, Mozart is reminded that he has not written an overture. He has his wife serve punch and tell him fairy tales throughout the night until it is finished. 'The ink was hardly dry on some of the pages when they were placed on the desks of the orchestra' (Wenzel Swoboda, double bass player in the orchestra).

1813 Paganini, 21, debuts at La Scala. 'His playing is truly *inexplicable*,' notes a critic.

1889 Handwritten copies of Tolstoy's latest tale begin circulating against his wishes in St Petersburg. *The Kreutzer Sonata* is inspired by a performance of Beethoven's Op. 47 and the author's private obsession: 'The question of sexual relations between husband and wife ... preoccupies me constantly.'

1986 The first opera based on a neurological case history, *The Man Who Mistook His Wife For a Hat*, opens in London, led by composer Michael Nyman from the keyboard.

1822 Schubert leaves his B minor symphony unfinished, apparently in emotional turmoil at the discovery that he has syphilis.

1826 Beethoven concludes his last String Quartet, Op. 135, scribbling at the head of the finale '... Must it be? it must be! it must be!'

1917 Leos Janáček, 63, in love with Kamila Stösslová, 25 and married, starts writing a string quartet that he names *The Kreutzer Sonata* after Tolstoy's tale of sexual anguish.

1925 *Paganini*, Léhar's opera on the fiddler, opens in Vienna.

1944 Copland's *Appalachian Spring*, depicting pioneer life in the West, is danced by Martha Graham at the Library of Congress, wins a Pulitzer Prize and becomes the best-loved modern American ballet.

1608 Girolamo Frescobaldi's inaugural recital as organist at St Peter's, Rome, draws a crowd of 30,000.

1828 Franz Schubert, about 'to eat some fish in the evening, suddenly threw his knife and fork on the plate as soon as he had tasted the first morsel, suggesting that he found this food immensely repellent and felt as though he had just taken poison. From that moment Schubert hardly ate or drank anything more, taking nothing but medicines. He tried to find relief by walking in the fresh air ...' – memoir by his brother, Ferdinand.

1932 Sergei Prokofiev plays the fifth and finest of his piano concertos, with Wilhelm Furtwängler conducting the Berlin Philharmonic.

1970 The cellist Mstislav Rostropovich, in a letter that *Pravda* refuses to publish, defends the outlawed Alexander Solzhenitsyn, who has found refuge in his home outside Moscow. He is immediately subjected to similar State persecution.

N · O · V · E · M · B · E · R

 1 NOVEMBER

1871 *Lohengrin* is the first Wagner opera to be seen in Italy. 'Mediocre impression,' notes Verdi.

1880 Gustav Mahler, 20 and depressed, becomes vegetarian. 'The moral effect of this way of life, with its voluntary castigation of the body, causing one's material needs to dwindle away, is enormous . . . I expect of it no less than the *regeneration* of humanity.'

1911 Scots soprano Mary Garden sells kisses for charity after Massenet's *Cendrillon* in Chicago. 'Believe me, she is some kisser,' gasps 'Tough' Darnum, a lucky bidder.

1972 Ezra Pound, revered but racist poet, pseudonymous music critic (as 'Walter Atheling'), author of an unorthodox harmony manual and composer of two anti-operas, *Le Testament de Villon* and *Cavalcanti*, dies in Venice two days after his 87th birthday.

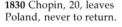 **2 NOVEMBER**

1830 Chopin, 20, leaves Poland, never to return.

1873 Brahms earns his loudest applause with *Variations on a theme by Haydn*. But the theme he has borrowed is not by Haydn: it is a mediaeval hymn, the 'St Antony Chorale'.

1960 Dmitri Mitropolous, 64, drops dead while conducting Mahler's Third symphony in a rehearsal at La Scala, Milan.

1979 The Salieri-Mozart inquest reopens in *Amadeus*, Peter Shaffer's play at the National Theatre, London, with the protagonists' music subtly adapted by Harrison Birtwistle.

1 NOVEMBER

2 NOVEMBER

3 NOVEMBER

 4 NOVEMBER

 5 NOVEMBER

1363 Guillaume de Machaut, 63, composer, diplomat and priest, to his 'sweetest love', Peronnelle: 'There is nothing in this world my body would not perform at your command, or in order to see you. For your perfect beauty and your exquisite sweetness draw me and my heart as a magnet draws iron . . . My sweetest heart, I am sending you the 11 ballades which you once saw, and which were made for you.'

1587 Samuel Scheidt is baptised at Halle, 97 years ahead of Handel.

1810 Rossini's first opera, *La cambiale di matrimonio*, is staged at Venice. He is 18 years old.

1882 Smetana's *Ma Vlast* (*My Country*), in praise of Czech landscape and history, is played in Prague.

1943 In Leningrad, Shostakovich hears his Eighth and . . .

1945 . . . Ninth Symphonies.

1827 Schubert, dying, applies for lessons in counterpoint.

1863 After attending the only part of *Les Troyens* that Berlioz lives to hear, Georges Bizet challenges a heckler, a conductor called Chéri, to a duel.

Fading Fauré

1876 'Seldom if ever has the entire musical world awaited a composer's first symphony with such tense anticipation' – Eduard Hanslick, on the symphonic debut of Johannes Brahms, 43, at Karlsruhe.

1924 'I did what I could. Now . . . let God judge!' are Fauré's last words.

1494 Hans Sachs is born in Nuremburg. 'In his youth he learned the cobbler's trade. Yet he also took great delight in poetry and mastersong . . . With tireless energy he applied himself to the art, achieving such perfection that he far surpassed all who preceded him and was likely to surpass all to come' (*Book of the Mastersinger's Art*, Altdorf, 1697: Wagner's source for his comic opera).

1938 The adagio from his first string quartet becomes Samuel Barber's best-known piece and America's favourite funeral dirge – in 1945 it announces the death of President Roosevelt – in its orchestral transcription, premiered over the NBC network by Arturo Toscanini.

1955 Rebuilt from bomb rubble, the Vienna State Opera reopens with *Fidelio* conducted by Karl Böhm.

1717 Bach, 32, is 'confined to the [Weimar] County Judge's place of detention for too stubbornly forcing the issue of his dismissal'. He is released and expelled from Weimar four weeks later.

1893 At 3 a.m. Peter Ilyich Tchaikovsky, 53, is carried off, allegedly by cholera. More probably, he took poison to avoid exposure in a high-placed homosexual scandal.

1936 'Sourly,' says Rachmaninov when asked how his Third symphony went down in Philadelphia.

1943 'O your little breasts
your soft breasts
sweetly smelling
twin fruits!
Ah! my hand is
eager . . .
O how your nipples
stand out . . .'
Catulli Carmina, vapidized verses of Catullus set by Carl Orff, receive their first performance in Leipzig.

1890 César Franck cries out on his deathbed: *'Mes enfants, mes pauvres enfants!'* It is understood that he is thinking of his musical progeny.

1901 At a dinner party in Vienna, Gustav Mahler meets his future bride, Alma, sitting between two of her many suitors, the artist Gustav Klimt and the theatre director Max Burckhard.

1928 Richard Strauss to Hugo von Hofmannsthal: 'I've had a good look again at the first act of *Arabella* . . . but the thing doesn't even begin to come to music and, to be perfectly frank, the characters don't interest me in the least . . .'

1934 Rachmaninov plays his *Rhapsody on a Theme of Paganini*, Stokowski conducting, in Baltimore.

1983 Germaine Tailleferre, 91, the only woman among *Les Six*, dies in Paris.

1890 Six months after being struck by a horse-drawn bus, César Franck, 67, expires. 'Winter and summer he was up at 5.30. The first two morning hours were generally devoted to composition – 'working for himself', he called it. About 7.30, after a frugal breakfast, he started to give lessons all over the capital, for to the end of his days this great man had to spend most of his time teaching piano to amateurs. All day long he went about on foot or by omnibus . . . and returned to his quiet abode on the Boulevard Saint-Michel in time for an evening meal. Although worn out with the day's work he still managed to find a few minutes to orchestrate or copy his scores' (Vincent D'Indy).

1924 Sergei Liapunov, 63, Rimsky-Korsakov's successor at the St Petersburg Conservatoire, ends his days as head of a Paris music school for Russian émigrés.

1926 Ira's emergency appendectomy cannot delay *Oh, Kay!*, third musical by the brothers Gershwin.
'Do, do, do
What you've done,
done, done
Before, Baby.'

6 NOVEMBER

 7 NOVEMBER

 8 NOVEMBER

9 NOVEMBER

10 NOVEMBER

11 NOVEMBER

1760 Haydn, 28, becomes engaged to Maria Anna Apollonia Keller, daughter of his landlord, though in love with her younger sister, Therese, a nun.

1881 Brahms plays his Second Piano Concerto at Budapest.

1901 Finding the resplendent opening movement 'absolutely repulsive', Rachmaninov performs his second piano concerto in C minor, his cousin Alexander Siloti conducting the Moscow Philharmonic. Dedicated to the neurotherapist who helped him overcome the public rejection of his First symphony, it becomes the 20th century's best-loved concerto.

1940 Joaquin Rodrigo's *Concierto de Aranjuez*, the most popular concert work for guitar, is premiered in Barcelona.

1483 Martin Luther is born at Eisleben. 'The fellow was like me,' says Wagner, 'had the writing itch, scribbled about everything.'

1668 François Couperin, who anagrammatizes his name to Pernucio to have his sonatas accepted in France, is born in Paris.

1904 Ferruccio Busoni plays his ambitious piano concerto with choral finale in Berlin. 'I hope to produce as perfect a work as is humanly possible,' he aspires. 'Noise, more noise, eccentricity and licentiousness,' carp the critics.

1906 Leipzig stages *The Wreckers* by militant English feminist Ethel Smyth.

1910 Elgar conducts Fritz Kreisler in his violin concerto at Queen's Hall, London, earning 'rapturous applause such as might have greeted the victor of Trafalgar'.

1898 Delius pays 500 francs for Gauguin's Tahitian nude *Nevermore*, delighting the artist since he bought it out of admiration not speculation. Poverty, 25 years later, forces him to sell.

1906 In Copenhagen, Carl Nielsen conducts his comic *Maskarade*, recognized as Denmark's national opera.

Priceless Rite

1918 As the Armistice is signed, Stravinsky, penniless in Switzerland, writes *Ragtime*.

1982 Stravinsky's draft of *The Rite of Spring* breaks all auction records, selling for £330,000 at Sotheby's to the Paul Sacher Collection in Basle.

1833 Alexander Porfir'yevich Borodin is born in St Petersburg, illegitimate son of a prince but named after one of his serfs. 'As a composer I wish to remain incognito. Music . . . for me is a rest and a pastime which distracts me from the absorbing duties that tie me to a professorial chair. I love the Academy of Medicine and my pupils' (self-definition).

1880 Wagner and King Ludwig meet for the last time. The King arrives 15 minutes late for his concert and, after hearing the prelude to *Parsifal*, insists that it be repeated. Wagner hands the baton to a colleague and walks out.

1931 Abbey Road, the London recording studio later immortalised by the Beatles, is opened by Sir Edward Elgar and the London Symphony Orchestra with the *Pomp and Circumstance* marches.

1843 Donizetti in Paris conducts *Dom Sebastian, King of Portugal*, his last opera. Asked which of his operas he thought the best he spontaneously replies: 'How can I say which? A father always has a preference for a crippled child, and I have so many . . .'

1868 On Friday 13th at Passy outside Paris, Rossini, 76, dies. 'My immortality? Do you know what will survive me? The third act of *Tell*, the second act of *Otello* and the *Barber of Seville*.'

1916 Septimus Kelly, 35, Australian composer, falls on a French battlefield.

1940 *Fantasia*, a collaboration between Walt Disney and Leopold Stokowski, whose tails are tugged tauntingly by Mickey Mouse, goes on release in New York, baptising a generation of babes in classical music.

1948 Arnold Schoenberg attacks Thomas Mann for having 'taken advantage of my literary property' in his novel *Doctor Faustus*, whose central figure is a composer using 'a system of 12 tones'.

1897 'Now *addio* my Verdi. As we were united in life, may God rejoin our spirits in Heaven' – Verdi loses Giuseppina, his companion for 50 years.

1900 Aaron Copland starts life in Brooklyn, fifth child of an immigrant who founded a department store.

1908 George Bernard Shaw's *Arms and the Man* is confected into Oscar Straus's *Chocolate Soldier* in Vienna.

1943 Leonard Bernstein, 25, takes over without rehearsal a coast-to-coast broadcast of Strauss's *Don Quixote* and a new suite by Miklós Rózsa. 'American success story,' proclaims the *New York Times* on its front page.

12 NOVEMBER

13 NOVEMBER

14 NOVEMBER

16 NOVEMBER

17 NOVEMBER

1667 'Home, and there find, as I expected, Mr Caesar and little Pelham Humphreys, lately returned from France and is an absolute Monsieur, as full of form and confidence and vanity, and disparages everything and everyone's skill but his own. But to hear how he laughs at all the king's music here . . .' (Samuel Pepys's diary). Humfrey, 20, is made a Gentleman of the Chapel Royal but dies at the age of 26.

1787 At lunch with visiting Parisians, Gluck, 73, defies doctor's orders and takes two liqueurs. That afternoon he suffers a fatal stroke.

1942 Daniel Barenboim is born of Ukrainian-Jewish piano teachers in Buenos Aires, where he makes his debut as a pianist at the age of seven.

1959 'Opera has no business making money' (Sir Rudolf Bing, director of the Met, to the *New York Times*).

1868 Cosima von Bülow, 30, leaves husband Hans and two small girls in Munich to consecrate her life to Richard Wagner, 55, by whom she already has two daughters and is pregnant with a son.

1900 Philadelphia founds an orchestra.

Caruso's conviction

1906 Enrico Caruso is arrested in the monkey house of Central Park Zoo, New York, and charged with molesting with his right elbow the left forearm of a Mrs Hannah Stanhope. He fails to appear in court, is found guilty and fined $10.

1959 The singing family Trapp are celebrated on Broadway in Rodgers' and Hammerstein's *The Sound of Music*.

1839 Verdi's first opera, *Oberto*, is staged at La Scala.

1891 Paderewski makes his US debut at Carnegie Hall. 'I had to play six piano concertos in one week, and a group of solos,' he complains.

1912 'Today, Sunday, while having an excruciating toothache, finished the music of *The Rite*' – Igor Stravinsky, Clarens [Switzerland].

1959 Heitor Villa-Lobos, 72, Brazilian composer, dies in Rio.

18 NOVEMBER

942 Odo, the Benedictine monk who names the notes of the diatonic scale with the letters A to G, dies at Cluny. 'You have insistently requested, beloved brothers, that I should communicate to you a few rules concerning music, these to be only of a sort which boys and simple persons may understand . . .' (Odo, *Enchiridion Muses*, c. 935).

1834 Bellini reports home: 'The best news is that Rossini (do not tell anyone) loves me very, very, very much . . . He told me I ought to stay in Paris and think no more about Italy.'

1836 W. S. Gilbert is born at 17 Southampton Street, The Strand, London. Aged 2, he is kidnapped at Naples by brigands.

1928 George Gershwin completes his tone poem: 'Imagine . . . an American visiting Paris, swinging down the Champs-Élysées on a mild sunny morning in May or June . . .'

 19 NOVEMBER

1828 At 3 p.m., six weeks short of his 32nd birthday, 'Schubert looked fixedly into the doctor's eyes, grasped at the wall with a feeble hand, and said slowly and seriously: "Here, here is my end!" '

1851 Louis Moreau Gottschalk, American pianist, so enchants the Queen of Spain that she bakes him a cake with her own fair hands. This makes her court pianist so jealous that he breaks the visitor's little finger.

1893 Dvořák starts a sonatina (Op. 100), inspired by a trip to the Minnehaha Falls, Minnesota.

1923 The jubilee of Budapest, a capital formed by the amalgamation of three neighbouring towns, is celebrated by premieres from Hungary's musical triumvirate: a *Festival Overture* by Dohnányi, Bartók's *Dance Suite* and Kodály's *Psalmus Hungaricus*, a setting of Psalm 55.

1936 A concert given by Beecham and the London Philharmonic at Ludwigshafen, Germany, is the first to be recorded on magnetic tape, an invention of the I. G. Farbenindustrie.

20 NOVEMBER

1805 A week after Napoleon enters Vienna, Beethoven presents *Fidelio* to a near-empty theatre.

1864 When Bruckner's Mass in D minor is sung at Linz Cathedral, the Bishop is so moved he is unable to pray.

1889 Gustav Mahler, 29, director of the Royal Budapest Opera, conducts his First symphony in two parts and five movements, one of which he removes after the frosty reception: 'My friends shunned me in terror. Not one of them dared to mention the work of its performance to me and I wandered about like a leper or an outlaw.'

1911 Six months after Mahler's death, Bruno Walter performs *Das Lied von der Erde* in Munich. 'What do you think?' Mahler once asked him. 'Is this bearable? Will people not do away with themselves after hearing it?'

 **18 NOVEMBER**

 19 NOVEMBER

 20 NOVEMBER

21 NOVEMBER

22 NOVEMBER

23 NOVEMBER

1695 'I, Henry Purcell, of the Citty [sic] of Westminster, gent., being dangerously ill as to the constitution of my body, but in good and perfect mind and memory (thanks be to God), doe by these presents publish and declare this to be my last Will and Testament' – Purcell, 36, dies within hours of writing these words: British music does not recover for two centuries.

1828 Schubert's estate is valued at 63 florins – less than £3. His funeral (second class) costs £27.

1874 Wagner, before noon of a 'thrice sacred memorable day', writes the last notes of the *Ring*.

1937 Shostakovich's Fifth symphony, 'a Soviet artist's response to just criticism', restores him to Stalin's favour. 'The Soviet listener rejects decadent, sombre or pessimistic art but responds enthusiastically to joyful, self asserting artistic declarations,' approves *Izvestia*.

1862 Verdi's *La forza del destino* is staged at St Petersburg.

1874 At 8.30 p.m. in Vienna, Bruckner completes his Fourth symphony.

1900 'The death of Sir Arthur Sullivan may be said without hyperbole to have plunged the whole empire in gloom' – *The Times*.

Serious Sullivan

1901 Composer Joaquin Rodrigo dawns at Sagunto, Valencia, and loses his sight at the age of three.

1913 Benjamin Britten is born at Lowestoft, Suffolk, youngest child of a dentist. He starts composing at five years old.

1928 'I have written only one masterpiece. That is *Bolero*. Unfortunately it contains no music' – Ravel's most performed work is danced in Paris.

1585 'As he dyd lyve, so also did he dy, in myld and quyet sort (O happy man)' reads the epitaph for Thomas Tallis, who composed obediently first for Roman rites then for Anglican.

1918 Schoenberg, despairing of public support for new music, founds in Vienna a Society for Private Musical Performances:
 The performances must be removed from the corrupting influence of publicity . . . [and] be unaccompanied by applause or demonstrations of disapproval.
 Virtuosity which makes the music not the end in itself but merely a means to an end will be avoided.
 To ensure equal attendance at each meeting, the programme will not be made known beforehand.
 Guests (foreign visitors excepted) shall not be admitted. Members will be required to abstain from giving any public report of the performances.

1933 Polish composer Krzystof Penderecki chimes in at Debica.

1900 Scriabin's First symphony is heard in St Petersburg.

1907 Vitezslav Novak's opera *Lady Godiva*, extolling the bare-all equestrianism of an 11th-century English noblewoman, is seen in Prague.

1956 Newly named principal conductor at La Scala, Guido Cantelli, 36, is killed in an air crash near Orly Airport, Paris.

1966 Rosemary Brown, a psychically-gifted South London housewife, receives from the spirit of J. S. Bach a Prelude in E flat major that some scholars are prepared to accept as a posthumous 49th of his immortal 48 Preludes and Fugues.

1835 Robert Schumann, 25, and Clara Wieck, 16, share their first kiss on her father's doorstep. 'I thought I would faint,' she informs him later. 'Everything went blank and I could barely hold the lamp that was lighting your way out.'

1882 In a ruse to defeat copyright pirates, Gilbert and Sullivan's *Iolanthe* is the first show ever to open simultaneously on both sides of the Atlantic.

1896 Virgil Thomson, critic and composer, signs in at Kansas City. 'On my second day at school I got into a fight,' he recalls.

1934 'Nobody who reads it can overlook the deep ethical quality that inspired its creator,' writes Wilhelm Furtwängler as he strives to convince Nazi Germany not to ban Hindemith's *Mathis der Maler*. His article provokes a demonstration of support at his Berlin concert that night, following which he is stripped of his conductorships and placed in quarantine.

1760 Haydn marries miserably in St Stephen's Cathedral, Vienna. 'His wife was domineering, unfriendly and spendthrift; he had to hide his income from her. She was also a bigot, always inviting clergymen to dinner' (Griesinger).

1898 Czech violinist Jan Kubelik is hailed as the new Paganini at his Vienna debut.

1944 Yehudi Menuhin plays the sonata he has commissioned from the ailing Bartók: 'I knew he was in financial straits . . . Little did I foresee that he would write for me one of the masterpieces of all time.'

1959 Albert Ketèlby, composer of *In a Persian Market* and similar exotica, ends his days on the Isle of Wight, aged 84.

24 NOVEMBER

25 NOVEMBER

26 NOVEMBER

1474 Guillaume Dufay, mid-70s*, foremost Franco-Flemish polyphonist, summons *in articulo mortis* eight choristers of Cambrai Cathedral to sing, very softly, a motet of his own composition to the words, *Miserere tui labentis Dufay'* ('Have mercy on your dying Dufay').

1896 Richard Strauss conducts in Frankfurt *Also Sprach Zarathustra*, his symphonic poem inspired by Nietzsche's super-humanic ideal. 'By far the most important of my pieces,' he tells his wife; 'the most perfect in form, the richest in content, the most individual in character.'

1926 After audience uproar at the première of *The Miraculous Mandarin*, the Mayor of Cologne, Konrad Adenauer, bans Bartók's modernist pan-tomime and calls for the dismissal of its conductor, Eugen Szenkar.

* Latest research on Dufay gives his birth as *c.* 1398.

1863 'The day we found each other and were united in *Liebes-Todesnot'* – Cosima von Bülow and Richard Wagner secretly seal 'our vow to live for each other alone'.

1867 After hearing it a second time, Edvard Grieg, 24, withdraws his only symphony, marking the score 'never to be per-formed'.

Cosima

1983 Messiaen's only opera, the five-hour *St François d'Assise*, staged in Paris, is intended as the climax of his career.

1643 Monteverdi, 76, dies in Venice.

1797 Gaetano Donizetti is born at Bergamo.

1825 Italian opera reaches the United States in a *Barber of Seville* at the Park Theatre, New York, star-ring Manuel Garcia, Ros-sini's original Almaviva. In the audience sits Lorenzo da Ponte, 76, Mozart's librettist.

1914 'I was lying on the dead Cossack who had wounded me . . .' Violin-ist Fritz Kreisler recounts his combat experiences in the *New York Times*.

1924 Giacomo Puccini, 65, dies in a Brussels clinic after surgery for throat cancer.

1623 Thomas Weelkes, 47, composer, Chichester Cathedral organist, 'notorious swearer and blasphemer', expires in London. 'Weelkes is the true English artist. He is an individualist as opposed to the Latin artist who tends to be a member of a school and as opposed to the inartistic Englishman whose thinking and feeling are arranged for him by convention' (Gustav Holst).

1654 Lully's ballet *Le Temps* wins him a post at Louis XIV's court.

1868 William Roberts, born in Liverpool, discovers music while working as a bank clerk. It makes him 'a new man in earnest': he takes the name Ernest Newman on becoming a professional music critic in 1905.

1915 *The In-Laws*, an opera by Hindemith's future father-in-law, is staged at Frankfurt.

1927 'I finish one work after another, as if I were soon to settle my account with life,' writes Janáček, 74, desperately fighting time.

1 DECEMBER

 2 DECEMBER

D * E * C * E * M * B * E * R

---

1 DECEMBER

1615 Johann (Hans) Bach, 60-ish, the family's earliest known musician, dies at the court of Nürtingen, where he is violinist and jester. His portrait bears the legend:

'Hie siehst du geigen/
Hansen Bachen
Wenn du er hörst/so
mustu lachen ...'

'Here you see Hans Bach;
When you hear him, you have to laugh.'

1707 Jeremiah Clarke, 33, shoots himself mortally in the churchyard of St Paul's Cathedral, where he is organist, for love of 'a very beautiful lady of a rank far superior to his own.'

1902 Carl Nielsen conducts his Second symphony, *The Four Temperaments*, named after a comic painting he has seen while drinking in a Zealand village pub.

1930 Kaikhosru Sorabji, 38, gives the only performance of his *Opus Clavicembalisticum* in Glasgow. Claimed to be the longest work for piano, its passacaglia alone boasts 81 variations.

1950 E. J. Moeran, 55, English composer, drowns in the River Kenmare, County Kerry.

---

2 DECEMBER

1608 Monteverdi, 41, resting in Cremona, is summoned back to the Court of Mantua. He replies: 'From my recent hard labours I have developed a bad head and itching all over my body which burns so fiercely that neither by applying cauteries and taking medicine, nor by bloodletting and other drastic remedies, have I got much better. My father ascribes my bad head to overwork and the itching to the air of Mantua

which, he suspects, will soon be the death of me.'

1877 Liszt stages at Weimar Saint-Saëns' opera, *Samson et Dalila*.

1883 Brahms' Third symphony in Vienna. Hanslick extols: 'If one were to call Brahms' first symphony the *Appassionata* and the second the *Pastoral*, then the new symphony might well be called the *Eroica*.'

1965 The University of California, Los Angeles, presents *Playable Music No. 4* by Nam June Paik. When Joseph Byrd interprets the composer's direction to 'cut your left arm very slowly with a razor (more than 10cm)', someone in the audience shouts: 'Encore! Use your throat!'

1721 Bach takes a second wife, Anna Magdalena.

1903 At Ingrave, Essex, Ralph Vaughan Williams, 29, starts collecting folksongs. His first is called 'Bushes and Briar'.

1908 England's first successful symphony, Elgar's A-flat major, is conducted in Manchester by Hans Richter, who declares it 'the greatest symphony of modern times, *and not only in this country.*'

Vaughan Williams

1923 Evangelia Kalogeropoulos is delivered in New York of a 12½-pound daughter, Cecilia Sophia Anna Maria, later to be known as Maria Callas. The diva celebrates her birthday on December 2nd; her estranged mother remembers giving birth on the 4th; school records cite the 3rd.

1732 'Life is a jest, and all
things show it:
I thought so once,
and now I know
it.'
John Gay's self-epitaph in Westminster Abbey.

1881 Tchaikovsky's violin concerto is played in Vienna by Adolph Brodsky. 'It poses for the first time the appalling notion that there can be works of music that stink to the ear' gripes Eduard Hanslick.

1902 Feodor Ignatievich Stravinsky, 59, heroic bass and father of composer Igor, makes his last public appearance in St Petersburg. 'The body was frozen like a piece of meat, dressed in evening clothes, and photographed' (Igor Stravinsky to Robert Craft).

1976 Benjamin Britten, 63, closes his eyes at Aldeburgh: 'Night and silence – these are two of the things I cherish most.'

1791 'Süssmayr was standing by the bedside and on the counterpane lay the *Requiem* ... As he looked over the pages for the last time, he said, with tears in his eyes, "Did I not tell you that I was writing this for myself?"' – Moments before 1 a.m. Mozart, 35, breathes his last.

1791 Haydn, in London, awakes to '... a fog so thick that one might have spread it on bread.'

1830 Berlioz's *Symphonie Fantastique* is performed in Paris. 'The best part is a Witches' Sabbath in which the Devil reads the mass and the liturgy is parodied with the most horrifying, bloodiest grotesqueries. It is a farce which gaily releases in us all the hidden snakes we carry in our hearts. My neighbour in the next seat, a talkative young man, showed me the composer, who stood at the far end of the hall, in a corner of the orchestra, playing the kettledrums – for the drum is his instrument' (Heinrich Heine).

1927 Janáček's *Glagolitic Mass* is sung in Brno.

 **3 DECEMBER**

 4 DECEMBER

 5 DECEMBER

6 DECEMBER

7 DECEMBER

8 DECEMBER

1821 Beethoven completes his Op. 109 Piano Sonata.

1950 The first US President to order a nuclear attack turns on a *Washington Post* critic who disparaged his daughter's musicality: 'Mr Hume, I have just read your review of Margaret's concert ... Some day I hope to meet you. When that happens, you'll need a new nose, a lot of beefsteak for black eyes and perhaps a supporter below' – Harry S. Truman.

1964 'Our last day rehearsing [*Mikrophonie*] in Cologne, Stockhausen's wife finds a few things being used as instruments that have been missing from her kitchen recently' (Hugh Davies, *Mikrophonie i Diary*).

1982 Herbert von Karajan cancels all recordings, tours and festival appearances with the Berlin Philharmonic Orchestra over its refusal to accept a female clarinettist, Sabine Meyer.

1732 The first Covent Garden theatre is built by John Rich with profits from *The Beggar's Opera*.

1791 Mozart's coffin is carried by Salieri, Süssmayr and others to a mass grave in St Marx churchyard, outside Vienna.

1898 Rimsky-Korsakov's murderous *Mozart and Salieri* is staged in Moscow.

1939 Jascha Heifetz performs in Cleveland the concerto he commissioned from William Walton.

1849 Opening at Naples, the set of Verdi's *Luisa Miller* promptly collapses, thanks, it is said, to the machinations of a jealous local composer adept in the dark arts of the *jettatore*.

1865 Some 60 miles north of Helsinki, Johan Julius Christian Sibelius is born, son of a doctor who soon dies of typhus. 'Few can have had so sad a childhood as I did' he tells his fiancée.

1881 During the second Viennese performance of *Tales of Hoffmann*, 384 members of the audience are burned to death in a blaze that destroys the Ring Theatre. The opera is not staged again in Vienna for 20 years.

1939 James Galway, golden flautist, draws breath in Belfast. 'Many of the people living in or around Carnalea Street, including my dad, didn't think of themselves as working-class but as the workless class.'

1980 John Lennon, 40, ex-Beatle, is shot dead by a crazed fan, Mark Chapman, outside his New York apartment.

1836 Glinka, 32, is hailed as Russia's first composer when *A Life for the Tsar* is seen in St Petersburg. Within a month he is made Kapellmeister of the Imperial Chapel.

1842 He is less instantly successful with *Ruslan and Lyudmila*.

1850 After five weeks' work, Schumann completes his *Rhenish symphony*.

Salome Strauss

1905 Richard Strauss's *Salome*, described by Cosima Wagner as 'absolute madness', opens uneventfully at Dresden.

1968 An oratorio by Hans Werner Henze dedicated to the slain Latin American guerrilla leader Che Guevara is called off when the Hamburg chorus refuses to sing beneath a red flag and the composer says he values world revolution more than a world premiere.

1896 Rimsky-Korsakov's completion of Mussorgsky's masterpiece *Boris Godunov* goes on stage in St Petersburg.

1908 Poetess Cécile Sauvage pens an ode in Avignon to her newborn baby's 'burgeoning soul'. He becomes the composer Olivier Messiaen.

1908 The Russian Symphony Orchestra of New York City premieres Scriabin's consummately erotic *Poème de L'Extase*, his Fourth symphony, which seeks to 'possess the Cosmos as a man possesses a woman.' 'The nerves of the audience were worn and racked as nerves are seldom assailed even in these days' notes the *New York Sun*.

1910 *The Girl of the Golden West*, Puccini's poker-playing opera of the '49-ers, opens at the Met with Caruso and Emmy Destinn as the lovers, and Toscanini conducting America's most prestigious world operatic premiere.

1803 'Decidedly ours is a prosaic century. On no other grounds can my wounded vanity account for the humiliating fact that no auspicious omens, no mighty portents ... gave notice of my coming. It is strange, but true, that I was born, quite unobtrusively, at La Côte Saint-André, between Vienne and Grenoble' – Hector Berlioz enters the world.

Bystander Berlioz

1823 Liszt, 12, arrives in Paris with his parents and takes room at the Hôtel d'Angleterre, opposite the offices of piano manufacturers Érard.

1908 Hours after Messiaen, US modernist Elliott Carter is born in New York.

1908 Delius directs *In a Summer Garden* at a Queen's Hall concert: 'I conducted without a catastrophe and that is about all – I don't think I shall try any more.'

9 DECEMBER

 10 DECEMBER

 11 DECEMBER

12 DECEMBER

 13 DECEMBER

14 DECEMBER

1527 Flemish madrigalist Adrian Willaert, 37, becomes the first *maestro di capella.*

1823 Liszt, 12, seeks admission to the Paris Conservatoire. Its Italian director, Cherubini, tells him he cannot admit foreigners.

1891 Richard Mühlfeld, whose account of the Mozart clarinet quintet inspires Brahms to write him a quintet and trio, performs both in Berlin.

1920 *La Valse*, Ravel's 'choreographic poem' of old Vienna, is heard in Paris but spurned by Diaghilev. 'It's a masterpiece,' he says, 'but it's not a ballet. It's a painting of a ballet.'

1823 Rossini, dreadfully seasick, reaches England.

1890 'For 40 years I have wanted to write a comic opera, and for 50 years I have known *The Merry Wives of Windsor* and yet the usual *buts* that are always present prevented me from fulfilling my wish. Now Boito has swept away all the *buts* and written me a comedy for music the like of which has never been seen. I am amusing myself composing it,

without any plans. I don't even know if I shall finish it. I repeat, I am amusing myself' – Verdi, reflecting on *Falstaff*.

1895 In Berlin, Gustav Mahler conducts, at his own expense and with the worst migraine of his life, his Second symphony, the *Resurrection*. 'Afterwards I saw grown men weeping and youths falling on each other's necks,' reports his sister.

1930 Stravinsky's *Symphony of Psalms*, 'composed for the glory of God and dedicated to the Boston Symphony Orchestra' on its 50th anniversary, is accidentally premiered in Brussels, the Boston debut having been set back a week by conductor Koussevitsky's indisposition.

1788 Carl Philipp Emanuel Bach, 74, architect of the keyboard sonata, dies in Hamburg where he has been cantor for 20 years. 'He is the father, we are the children,' writes Mozart.

1924 The first orchestral work to incorporate recorded sound (a disc of a nightingale's call), Respighi's *Pines of Rome*, is performed there.

1925 *Wozzeck*, Alban Berg's first opera, opens at the Berlin State Opera after 137 rehearsals led by Erich Kleiber. Fighting breaks out in the aisles and the composer is called all manner of critical names from 'inspired genius' to 'a swindler who endangers the musical

community' and 'poisoner of the spring of German music'. 'If it pleases people so much,' mutters Berg as he leaves the first night banquet, 'there must be something wrong with it.'

1826 At the largest so-called *Schubertiad*, Johann Vogl sings more than thirty lieder, 'and poor Franz Schubert had to accompany him endlessly so that his short and fat fingers would hardly obey him any longer.'

1888 'The Sultan Schariar, persuaded of the falseness and faithlessness of women, has sworn to put to death each of his wives after the first night. But the Sultana Scheherazade saved her life by interesting him in tales, which she told him during 1,001 nights ...' Rimsky-Korsakov conducts his instantly successful *Scheherazade*.

1899 At 3.00 a.m. Debussy completes his *Nocturnes*.

1934 A musician in the Rio de Janeiro Opera orchestra shoots and kills conductor Franco Paol-antonio during his performance of *Fedora*.

1941 The Red Army recaptures the Tchaikovsky Museum at Klin; *Izvestia* reports that German soldiers had excreted beside a portrait of Beethoven.

1877 'The darkest day of Bruckner's life'. He conducts his *Wagner Symphony*, the third, and most of the Viennese audience walk out.

1886 All the lights go out in Brussels as Eugène Ysaÿe premieres Franck's violin sonata. Unperturbed, he plays two movements from memory.

Beethoven's birthplace

1921 Camille Saint-Saëns, 86, enjoys a performance of Delibes' *Lakmé* at the Algiers Opera, returns to the Hôtel L'Oasis and dies peacefully in his sleep.

1940 'For 30 years, bald parchment-faced Austrian-born composer Arnold Schoenberg has written music so complicated that only he and a couple [of] other fellows understand what it is all about' – *Time* magazine on the premiere of Schoenberg's violin concerto.

1538 'If God gives us such boons in life, which is but a vale of trials and tears, what will it be like hereafter!' – Martin Luther, after a concert at his home.

1770 Beethoven is baptized in Bonn; he was probably born on the previous day.

1930 Philip Heseltine, 36, perspicacious critic who composed pseudonymously as Peter Warlock, 'choosing a moment when his mistress was away from the flat ... put the cat outside the door so that it should not be a fellow victim, and turned on the gas' (Anthony Powell).

1946 Following his denazification, Wilhelm Furtwängler explains that he remained to conduct in the Third Reich because: 'when was the music of Beethoven more needed than in Himmler's Germany?'

15 DECEMBER

 16 DECEMBER

 17 DECEMBER

18 DECEMBER

 19 DECEMBER

 20 DECEMBER

1737 Antonio Stradivari, the greatest violin-maker, dies in his nineties in Cremona. 'He was tall and thin. Habitually covered with a cap of white wool in winter, and of cotton in summer, he wore over his clothes an apron of white leather' (Fétis).

1838 Paganini urges Berlioz 'kindly to accept, as a token of my homage, 20,000 francs.' Berlioz replies: 'O worthy and great artist ... Words fail me; I shall rush to embrace you as soon as I can leave my bed.'

1892 Bruckner's Eighth entrances Vienna, though arch-critic Eduard Hanslick calls it 'a nightmarish hangover'.

1908 Playing Debussy's *Children's Corner* in Paris, Harold Bauer discovers a savage parody of *Tristan* in the *Golliwogg's Cake Walk*.

1890 *The Queen of Spades*, Tchaikovsky's opera on Pushkin's three-card trick, triumphs in St Petersburg.

1935 Alban Berg, critically ill with a blood infection, is given a transfusion. He thanks the donor, saying, 'I hope this will not turn me into an operetta composer.'

1937 Ravel undergoes unsuccessful brain surgery.

Berg and Webern

1822 Beethoven undertakes to write a Ninth Symphony for the Philharmonic Society in London, 'although the price given by the English cannot be compared with those paid by other nations.'

1862 Borodin becomes lecturer in chemistry at the St Petersburg Academy of Medicine. 'The only signs of impatience he showed were provoked by our [student] negligence. "Little father," he would then say ... "How can you make such bad smells in such a beautiful laboratory?"'

1881 'Deafness is no joke for a musician,' says afflicted Smetana.

1982 Arthur Rubinstein, 95, pianist and *bon vivant*, passes on in Switzerland in the loving company of a young Englishwoman. 'Since my 90th birthday I have been living the happiest time of my life ...'

1908 As Schoenberg's second string quartet is played in the Bösendorfersaal, Vienna, 'Elegant ladies uttered cries of pain, raising hands to their delicate ears. Elderly gentlemen wept tears of anguish at the dissonances.'

1911 Dear Berg,
I am sending you a little Christmas present – Kant's letters. Don't be angry with me, but I feel I must do this. There are few things as marvellous as Christmas. Think about it: after almost 2,000 years, the night a great man was born is celebrated by almost all men on earth as a moment when everyone says only kind things and wishes to do good. That *is* wonderful. Shouldn't Beethoven's birthday be celebrated in the same way? . . .'

Your Webern.

1939 Prokofiev's *Zdravitza*, a salute for Stalin's 60th birthday (with Russian, Ukrainian, Byelorussian, Kurd, Mari and Mordva texts), is slavishly performed in Moscow.

1808 In a four-hour concert at the Theater an der Wien, Beethoven squeezes the first performance of his Fifth and Sixth symphonies between his fourth piano concerto, parts of the Mass in C, the aria *'Ah! perfido'*, the Choral Fantasia and some piano improvisations.

1858 'Descended of a long line of musicians worthy of the living tradition of the fatherland, Giacomo Puccini, who . . . re-affirmed in pure and lively forms the glorious primacy of our national art, was born here' – civic inscription at Puccini's birthplace at Lucca.

1894 Debussy's *Prélude à l'après-midi d'un faune*, orchestral evocation of a Mallarmé poem, is performed almost unnoticed in Paris. The poet says: 'I didn't expect anything like that.'

1981 Chancellor Helmut Schmidt of West Germany plays third piano in Mozart's triple concerto with Christoph Eschenbach and Justus Frantz at Abbey Road studios, London. He is the first serving head of government to make a commercial piano recording.

1806 Franz Clement, director of the orchestra at the Theater an der Wien, plays Beethoven's violin concerto, the ink still wet on the page.

1857 Wagner hires a chamber orchestra to play *Träume [Dreams]*, one of two 'Studies for *Tristan and Isolde'*, beneath the window of his mistress Mathilde Wesendonck, whose 29th birthday it is.

1893 Richard Strauss premieres Engelbert Humperdinck's children's opera *Hansel und Gretel*, which Siegfried Wagner proclaims the most important opera since his father's.

1917 Rachmaninov, 44, leaves Russia forever. Noone sees him off but Chaliapin sends caviare and home-baked white bread for the journey.

1976 'To be himself, a man must be born anew every day' – Pierre Boulez, interview in *Le Monde*.

21 DECEMBER

 22 DECEMBER

 23 DECEMBER

24 DECEMBER

 25 DECEMBER

 26 DECEMBER

1453 John Dunstable, eminent composer, astrologer and mathematician, dies; he is buried in St Stephen's, Walbrook, London. These are the only known facts of his life.

1818 Finding the organ out of order at St Nicholas Church, Oberdorf, the curate, Joseph Mohr, asks Franz Xaver Gruber to set a *Weinachtslied* for voices and guitar. The result is *Stille Nacht*, 'Silent Night', sung at Midnight Mass.

1837 Francesca Gaetana Cosima Liszt is born illegitimate at 2 p.m. to Countess Marie d'Agoult and Franz Liszt in a hotel room in Como; she observes her birthday on Christmas Day.

1871 *Aïda* becomes flesh at the Khedival Opera, Cairo. Verdi, two weeks earlier, is 'so disgusted, so revolted, so irritated that I would a thousand times set fire to the score without a sigh! Shall I?'

1935 Crying 'Ein Auftakt [An upbeat]!' Alban Berg expires at 50.

1734 Bach sets off his *Christmas Oratorio*, serialised in six parts at the two main Leipzig churches over the next twelve days.

1750 Handel sends exotic plants to cheer the ailing Telemann.

1845 The Bach dynasty comes to an end in Wilhelm Friedrich Ernst, 86, teacher of music in Berlin to the princes of Prussia.

1870 On her 33rd birthday, her first as Wagner's wife, Cosima is awoken by the *Siegfried Idyll*, his 'symphonic birthday greeting', played by a small orchestra stationed on the staircase of their Tribschen house. 'Now let me die,' she cries. 'Easier to die for me than to live for me,' replies Wagner.

1672 The world's first public concerts are announced in the *London Gazette '* . . . at Mr John Banister's House over against the George Tavern in Whyte Fryers, this present Monday, will be musick performed by excellent Masters, beginning at four o'clock in the afternoon and every afternoon for the future precisely at the same hour.' Tickets are one shilling each, and ale is served throughout.

1693 François Couperin, 25, is appointed *organiste du roi* at Versailles.

1767 In *Alceste*, Gluck cleanses opera of 'all those abuses introduced either by the mistaken vanity of singers or the excessive complaisance of composers . . . I have striven to restrict music to its true office of serving poetry by means of expression and by following the development of the story without the interruption of superfluous ornaments.'

1830 Donizetti makes his mark internationally with *Anna Bolena*, staged in Milan and soon after in Paris and London.

1831 *Norma*, Bellini's masterpiece, flops at Milan.

1914 In the dark winter of War, Ferruccio Busoni reads to his family the libretto of *Doktor Faust*: 'He alone is happy who looks to the future.'

27 DECEMBER

1875 Wagner dreams that the Queen of Prussia is his mother.

1898 Richard Strauss completes *A Hero's Life*.

1927 *'Ol' Man River'* is first heard when Jerome Kern's *Show Boat*, lyrics by Oscar Hammerstein II, opens in New York.

1944 Mrs Amy Beach, the first American woman to have a symphony performed, dies in New York, aged 77.

28 DECEMBER

1808 A *Liedertafel*, a gathering of men to eat, drink and sing four-part harmonies, is formed by Goethe's friend Zelter in Berlin.

1879 At 7 a.m. in a hotel room at 45 East 20th Street, New York, Arthur Sullivan recomposes *The Pirates of Penzance*, the only G & S show to be premiered in America. He left the music in England but rewrites it from memory three days before the opening.

1908 Eva Wagner, 41, fourth daughter of Richard and Cosima, weds the British proponent of German racial supremacy, Houston Stewart Chamberlain, and instals him at Bayreuth. 'Our misery began with Eva's marriage,' reflects one of her sisters.

1937 'I still had so much music to write,' sighs the dying Ravel, 62.

1963 Acute pancreatitis kills Paul Hindemith, 68.

29 DECEMBER

1708 J. S. Bach, 23, baptises the eldest of his 20 children, Catharina Dorothea.

1823 At the request of King George IV, to whom he is presented in Brighton, Rossini sings one of his *buffo* arias in a light falsetto, outraging courtiers who think he is a *castrato*.

1893 Debussy's String Quartet is played in Paris, Ysaÿe leading.

1961 'No good opera plot can be sensible, for people do not sing when they are feeling sensible' – W. H. Auden.

27 DECEMBER

28 DECEMBER

29 DECEMBER

30 DECEMBER

 31 DECEMBER

1877 'Brahms's Second Symphony extends its warm sunshine to connoisseurs and laymen alike. It belongs to all who long for good music, whether they are capable of grasping the most difficult or not' – Eduard Hanslick.

1905 Forced by a Viennese rival to open on the night before New Year's Eve, Franz Lehár triumphs with *The Merry Widow*.

Hanslick homage

1948 *Scott of the Antarctic*, a film of the fatal 1912 polar expedition, is screened in London with music by Ralph Vaughan Williams that forms the basis for his Seventh Symphony, the *Sinfonia Antartica*.

1961 In Moscow, 25 years after he removed it from rehearsal for fear of Stalin's wrath, Shostakovich's Fourth symphony is finally performed. 'Let them eat it,' mutters the composer.

1815 Schubert, an 18-year-old schoolmaster, has in the course of this year composed 145 songs, two symphonies, two masses, a string quartet in G minor and four stage works.

1831 Bellini reports: 'My poor *Norma* has been persecuted so cruelly, they tried to annihilate her at birth; all the papers are shouting fiasco fiaschissimo ... But the most diabolical intrigues cannot disguise the truth for long; in the end it will shine forth in its true light.'

1865 Verdi: 'I have heard the overture to *Tannhäuser* by Wagner. He's mad!!!'

1872 'R. not well, wraps himself in blankets – a dismal spectre is hovering over us – yesterday a huge spider crawled out of his bed – in the morning! ... It is nearly 12 o'clock as I write this; this year is ending gloomily and the new one lies gloomily in front of us; R. is weary of life, and I can only follow behind him, suffer with him, not help him! ... So at this midnight hour let me humbly accept as deserved whatever the coming year may bring, however hard, and may God give me the grace to do good!' – Cosima Wagner.

1876 Tchaikovsky thanks his unseen benefactress, Nadezhda von Meck: 'It is a great comfort to a musician to know that there exists a handful of people – of whom you are one – who are genuine and passionate lovers of music ...'.

1908 Prokofiev, 17, makes his debut playing six piano pieces in St Petersburg. 'It seemed as if the hall was ablaze and we were ready to perish alive in the fire of the music ... Something like this can be witnessed only once in a lifetime' (Vladimir Mayakovsky).

'Any musical innovation is full of danger to the whole
state, and ought to be prohibited . . . When modes of
music change, the fundamental laws of the state
always change with them.'

Plato, *The Republic*, Book IV.

 Abbreviations

NL =Interview with the author
G   =Grove's *Dictionary of Music and Musicians*,
        London, 1889.
NG   =*The New Grove Dictionary of Music and Musi-
        cians*, London, 1980.
CWD=Cosima Wagner's Diaries.

The author is grateful to the following copyright holders for permission to reprint brief text quotations:

R. Piper & Co. Verlag, Geoffrey Skelton and Harcourt Brace Jovanovich for *Cosima Wagner's Diaries*. London (Wm. Collins), 1978.

Alfred Knopf Inc. for N. Rimsky-Korsakov, *My Musical Life*, transl. Judah A. Joffe, New York, 1923/r. 1942.

Harper and Row Publishers and Solomon Volkov for *Testimony: the memoirs of Shostakovich*. London (Hamish Hamilton), 1979.

Faber & Faber Ltd and H. W. Henze for Hans Werner Henze, *Music and Politics*. London, 1982.

La Monte Young for *Composition 1960* No. 3.

Macmillan & Co. for dates in *The New Grove Dictionary of Music and Musicians*, ed. Stanley Sadie. London, 1980; and Nicolas Slonimsky for *Music since 1900*, 4th edition. London (Cassell), 1972.

And for the illustrations on the following pages:

21 Bibliothéque Nationale, Paris.
42 *Caruso Caricatures*, Michael Sisca (La Follia Di), New York.
139 Bibliothéque Nationale, Paris.
160 *La Revue Musicale*, Paris.
229 *La Revue Musicale*, Paris.
237 *Caruso Caricatures*, Michael Sisca (La Follia Di), New York.
241 The Mansell Collection, London.

All other illustrations are taken from the Lebrecht Collection, London.